A Nation of Immigrants?

A Brief Demographic History of Britain

David Conway

Civitas: Institute for the Study of Civil Society
London
Registered Charity No. 1085494

First Published April 2007

email: books@civitas.org.uk

ISBN 978-1-903386-58-3

Typeset by
Civitas

Printed in Great Britain by
The Cromwell Press
Trowbridge, Wiltshire

M

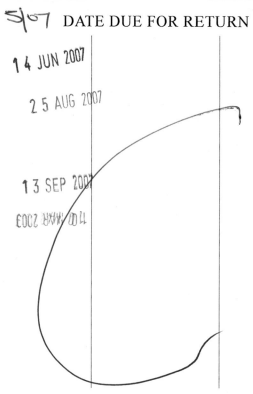

Contents

Author

David Conway is a Senior Research Fellow at Civitas. His publications include *A Farewell to Marx; Classical Liberalism: The Unvanquished Ideal; Free-Market Feminism; The Rediscovery of Wisdom* and *In Defence of the Realm: The Place of Nations in Classical Liberalism.*

Acknowledgements

This essay has greatly benefited from enormously helpful comments on an earlier draft received from Professor David Coleman, Dr Stephen Davies, Sir Andrew Green and Robert Whelan. The author is immensely grateful to them all for their comments and suggestions, as he is to Elizabeth P. Kearns for kindly having shown him a copy of an unpublished dissertation of hers on this subject.

All residual errors in the essay are, of course, entirely and solely the responsibility of its author.

We are grateful to MigrationWatch UK for a donation towards the cost of printing and distribution.

The legal and spiritual association of men of different creeds, callings, and classes in a nation, though often taken for granted, is a more wonderful miracle of cumulative human effort and wisdom than even the greatest achievement of science. For it enables millions who have never set eyes on one another to act together in peace and mutual trust. There can be no truer service than to preserve such a union, and prevent those millions from dissolving into antagonistic and destructive groups.

Sir Arthur Bryant, Spirit of England, 1982

1

Introduction

For some years now, a highly polarised, fiercely argued and still by no means concluded debate has been taking place between politicians, social policy theorists and other opinion-formers as to how desirable has been the recent scale of immigration to this country, especially, but not entirely, that from non-EU countries. In response to those who have voiced misgivings about the current scale of immigration, its apologists and advocates have often claimed it to be nothing new. According to them, Britain has always been a nation of immigrants.

One prominent public figure who has made this claim in recent years is the former Labour minister with special responsibility for immigration, the erstwhile MP Barbara Roche. She first did so in September 2000 in a speech at a conference on the future of labour migration to the UK organised by the Institute for Public Policy Research. In her speech, the then junior minister argued that Britain should adopt towards immigration a more relaxed approach than it had done in recent times since there was a need to facilitate the entry of more foreign workers. They were alleged to be needed partly to redress the country's ageing work force and partly to meet reputed labour shortages in a range of jobs, from information technology, through teaching and nursing, to catering and agriculture. Roche concluded her speech by saying that: 'This country is a country of migrants and we should celebrate the multi-cultural, multi-racial nature of our society, and the very positive benefits that migration throughout the centuries has brought.'[1]

Roche repeated this claim in a contribution she made to a Home Office Research Paper published in 2001 under the title *Migration: an economic and social analysis*. There, after claiming the country had always benefited from its immigrants because their self-selection meant that they were 'more resourceful, entrepreneurial and ambitious than the norm', she went on to state that 'the UK is a nation of immigrants'. Elsewhere in this report it is claimed that 'Britain is a country of immigration and emigration ...[and] the British population is now, as it has always been, the result of successive influxes of migrants'.[2]

Roche further repeated the claim in an article entitled 'Beat the backlash' published in *Progress* in 2004. In this article, Roche identified and suggested responses to several challenges facing those like her who favoured the more relaxed approach towards immigration that had by then become official government policy. One such challenge, claimed Roche, was 'to embrace our past as a nation of immigrants. History should not be all about kings and queens, dates and battles, but should look at how immigration is firmly entwined with any notion of what it is to be British.'[3]

In arriving at her view, it is possible the erstwhile minister had been influenced by a 1996 publication of the Commission of the Racial Equality called *Roots of the Future: Ethnic Diversity in the Making of Britain*. This publication was no less adamant than Roche in claiming ethnic diversity to be nothing new to Britain:

> People with different histories, cultures, beliefs, and languages have been coming here since the beginning of recorded time. Logically, therefore, everyone who lives in Britain today is either an immigrant or the descendant of an immigrant.[4]

A similar claim has recently been reiterated in a history of immigration to this country published in 2004 under the title *Bloody Foreigners: The Story of Immigration to Britain*. At the very beginning of this book its author, Robert Winder, informs his readers that 'we are all immigrants: it simply depends how far back you go'.[5] Shortly afterwards, he explains what he meant by making this claim by remarking that: 'Ever since the first Jute, the first Saxon, the first Roman and the first Dane leaped off their boats and planted their feet on British mud, we have been a mongrel nation.'[6]

Such claims as those made by the CRE, Roche and Winder seek to offer the British public reassurance as to the current scale of immigration to Britain by suggesting there to be nothing new or out of the ordinary about it. Those seeking to offer such reassurance contend the present-day scale of immigration is rather to be welcomed. This is because, in their view, immigrants are likely to have more than average enterprise and drive. Hence, they are thought likely to add enough to the nation's stock of human capital so as to make their settlement as advantageous to the nation whom they join as it is to them personally. Such a claim might well have once held true, when, being difficult and hazardous, only the most determined and resourceful would-be migrants journeyed here from distant parts. There is less reason to accept the claim so uncritically in our present age of mass-transit, when no part of the country is more than a day's journey by air from practically anywhere else on the globe. Moreover, the view that Britain is a nation of immigrants suggests Britain has always experienced immigration on its present-day scale from time immemorial, which is by no means the case.

To appreciate just how different in scale post-war immigration to Britain has been from what it was in earlier times, compare the several statements just quoted that amount in effect to the claim that Britain has always been a nation of immigrants with what George Trevelyan said on the same subject almost a century ago, when the scale of post-war immigration could scarcely have been foreseen. He expressed his views on the matter in the introduction to his magnificent *History of England*, first published in 1926. Trevelyan began by first paying homage to what he acknowledged as being the enormous debt the country owes to the successive waves of settlers by whom it was first populated up to the Norman Conquest. He wrote:

> Britain has always owed her fortunes to the sea.... [H]er destiny was continually being decided by the boat-crews which ... floated to her shore. From Iberian and Celtic to Saxon and Danish settlers, from pre-historic and Phoenician traders to Roman and Norman overlords, successive tides of warlike colonists, the most energetic seamen, farmers and merchants of Europe, came by the wave-path to inhabit her, or to instil their knowledge and spirit to the older inhabitants. Her east coast lay obvious and open to Teuton and Scandinavian immigrants; her south coast to cultural influences from the Mediterranean by way of France. From Teuton and Scandinavian she acquired the more important part of her population and character and the root of her language; from the south she received the rest of her language, the chief forms of her culture, and much of her organising power.[7]

The clear acknowledgement Trevelyan offers here of the enormous debt that Britain owes to its earliest settlers accords fully with the sentiments expressed by the several quotations from more recent authors cited earlier. However, very soon after making his acknowledgement, Trevelyan quickly dispels any suggestion that, for the past thousand years, the country has undergone immigration on anything approaching that early scale. In the opening passage of the first of the six books into which he divides his history, entitled 'The Mingling of the Races: From the Earliest Times to the Norman Conquest', Trevelyan enters the following observation:

> It is a commonplace to say that the British are a people of mixed blood... [But] it may be as well to say, at the outset, that the entrance into our island of the races who people it today was completed in main at the time of the Norman Conquest. With that

4

event, which itself made less racial than social and cultural change, we come to an end of migratory invasions and forced entry behind the point of the sword. Since Hastings there has been nothing more catastrophic than a slow, peaceful infiltration of alien craftsmen and labourers—Flemings, Huguenots, Irish and others—with the acquiescence of the existing inhabitants of the island.[8]

Here, in the most unequivocal of terms, Trevelyan denies that, since the Norman Conquest, Britain has undergone immigration on a scale anything like as great, proportionately speaking, as that formed by the several waves it underwent up to and including that Conquest. Nor, might we add, has the scale of immigration to Britain between the Norman Conquest and the end of World War Two been anything like as great as that on which it has taken place during the six decades since the final edition of Trevelyan's history was published in 1945.

It is moot whether the economic and cultural contribution of Britain's more recent immigrants has been or is likely to be as great as that made by Britain's earlier immigrants. As a political society, Britain has, for a long time, been both stable as well as liberal and tolerant, comparatively speaking. It would be one thing for Britain to have acquired and to have been able to preserve its stable and benign political character because of, or at least in spite of, having had a history of large-scale and continuous immigration, which is something implied by those who claim that it is and has always been a country of immigrants. It would be quite another were Britain only to have been able to acquire and to preserve its stable, tolerant, and liberal character because, during the period in which it acquired and has possessed this character, it did not undergo immigration on a scale so large as that which has recently taken place. Suppose Britain had only been able to acquire and retain its stability and free and tolerant character because, during this period, it possessed a relatively homogenous demographic composition. Then, its ability to retain that character could well be under a far more severe threat from current levels of immigration than is made out by those who maintain that substantial immigration has always been a constant feature of Britain's demographic history from time immemorial.

Those who cherish Britain's comparative stability, freedom, and tolerance cannot afford to ignore the potential threat that is posed to it by the large-scale changes in its demographic composition now taking place as a result of recent large-scale immigration in combination with declining fertility among its indigenous population. A society must always find it harder to reproduce its political culture and to maintain its traditions the less deeply rooted its members become in it historically and ethnographically. Of late, there has been a growing realisation of the plausibility of some such claim in light of the discovery that all four suicide-bombers of 7 July 2005 were British-born, second-generation British Muslims who had grown up in Britain in highly segregated enclaves in which normal patterns of acculturation into mainstream British life have apparently become far harder to sustain. It is particularly in light of how quickly and recently many such enclaves have sprung up in Britain, and are continuing to grow apace, that all those who want to see Britain remain the stable, liberal, and tolerant country it has been for so long need to consider carefully how much truth or falsehood is contained in the claim that Britain is and has always been a nation of immigrants. The following brief synoptic overview of the history of migration to Britain, from the time the country was first populated up to the present, aims to provide the wherewithal for an informed opinion on this question.

2

Clarifying the Question at Issue

The following outline sketch of Britain's demographic history is intended to enable the reader to reach an informed opinion on how far Britain may accurately be described as being a nation or country of immigrants and descendants of immigrants. Since the claim can be understood in more than one way, before embarking on consideration of this history, it will be worth spelling out in what precise way the claim shall be understood here for purposes of determining how far Britain's demographic history bears it out or disconfirms it.

There is one way in which the claim that Britain is a nation of immigrants and descendants of immigrants may be understood in which, while stating a truth, what it asserts is trivial and wholly uninteresting. This is when what it is understood as asserting is only that all of Britain's past and present inhabitants either migrated there during their lifetimes or else descend from people who did. When understood in this way, the claim is obviously true. For it is indisputable that, at one time, Britain was entirely uninhabited. The same applies to Japan and Australia, however. Yet few would wish to characterise Japan today, or Australia as it was at the time of the arrival there of Captain Cook when its sole inhabitants were the Aborigines, as a country of immigrants and descendants of immigrants. Yet both countries at these stipulated times were just as much countries of immigrants and descendants of immigrants as Britain. Clearly, when it is made about Britain, those making the claim intend to imply that immigration has played a much greater role in fashioning its demography than it has done in the case of either Japan as it today or Australia as it was at the time of the arrival of the British. Consequently, when made about Britain, the claim needs to be construed in some other way.

There is a second and different way in which to understand the claim in which, far from stating an uninteresting trivial truth, what it asserts is something that manifestly could not be true. This is when it is understood as asserting all members of the British nation to have acquired their membership of it either by having immigrated to Britain, or, if born there, by being descended from ancestors who acquired their membership of it by having immigrated to Britain. When so understand, the claim manifestly could not possibly be true. For someone can only acquire membership of a nation by immigrating to its territory, after the nation already exists. Since no nation can exist anywhere without containing members, it follows that there can be no nation whose entire membership is composed of those who have joined it as immigrants or else by descending from people who acquired their membership of it in that fashion. Every nation, in other words, must necessarily contain at least some members who acquired their membership neither by immigrating to that nation's territory, nor by descent from ancestors who did. Hence Britain cannot possibly be correctly described as a nation of immigrants and descendants of immigrants, if what is meant by the claim is that the British are a nation all of whose members became such by immigrating to Britain or else by descending from ancestors who did become members of it by immigrating there. Accordingly, when Britain is claimed to be a nation of immigrants and descendants of immigrants, in order for the claim to stand any chance of being true, it needs to be construed as being intended in some other way than to assert all British citizens to have acquired that status either by having immigrated to Britain, or else by descending from ancestors who did do.

It would be uncharitable to suppose that anyone who has ever claimed Britain to be a nation of immigrants could have intended the claim in a sense that would have rendered it either a trivial and uninteresting truth or else a manifest falsehood. Therefore, a principle of interpretative charity obliges us to try and find some third way in which to construe it where what it asserts is neither of these things. There is a third way the claim admits of being understood in which what it asserts is neither obviously true nor obviously false. It will be as so construed that shortly Britain's demographic history will be considered to see how far it bears out or disconfirms the claim when so construed. This third way of construing the claim involves understanding it to be asserting that the majority of Britain's citizens, not all of them, acquired that status by having immigrated to Britain or else by descending from people who acquired that status through having immigrated to Britain. When understood so, what the claim asserts is that only a minority of Britain's citizens have any ancestral roots there that go back to a time before it was a unitary state or even contained any of the several constituent states and principalities from whose union the unitary state that is Great Britain has been formed. It is to ascertain how much truth or falsity there is in the claim that Britain is a nation of immigrants and descendants of immigrants, when it is so construed, that its demographic history will now be considered to see how far it bears out or disconfirms the claim.

3

From the Stone Age to
The Roman Conquest

The last Ice Age ended approximately 13,000 years ago. At its peak, some 5,000 years earlier, a period known as the Last Glacial Maximum (LGM), the landmass that is Britain was an uninhabited and uninhabitable polar desert, as indeed was the rest of northern Europe. Britain and Europe were directly connected by land without any intervening sea, because the sea level then was so much lower than at present as a result of these lower temperatures having locked up as ice-sheets so much potential sea-water. Approximately 15,000 years ago, the temperatures in Europe north of the Alps had risen sufficiently to permit the return of plant and animal life, which had previously flourished there during several earlier inter-glacial periods. Following in the wake of its return came a small number of members of the hominid species *homo sapiens sapiens*. This hominid species is that from which all present-day humans are thought to descend. During the preceding Ice Age, the cold temperatures had confined them to the more temperate southerly regions of Europe into which they are thought to have first spread approximately 43,000 years ago from that region in central Africa in which the species is thought to have first originated some 200,000 years ago.

Of the human hunter-gatherers who followed the returning plant and animal life into northern Europe, some eventually made their way as far north and west as Britain. Evidence of their former presence there in the form of their skeletal remains has been found in Gough's Cave, Somerset, which date back some 12,000 years. Such early human inhabitants of Britain, however, were by no means the first humans ever to have lived in Britain, let alone the first hominids to have done so. Human skeletal remains some 31,000 years old have been found in Keat's Cavern, South Devon, and others discovered in Paviland in the Gower Peninsula that date back some 26,000 years. Some of these very earliest human inhabitants of Britain may well have resided there concurrently with other hominid species, most notably, the so-called 'Neanderthals'. This species is thought to have become extinct some 30,000 years ago. Neanderthal skeletal remains have been found in Britain in places such as Lynford in Norfolk. The very earliest hominid skeletal remains to be discovered in Britain were found in Boxgrove Quarry, Sussex, and date back half a million years.

Current scholarly opinion is divided on whether there was a continuous human presence in Britain during a 1,500-year-long spell of extreme cold that returned to the northern hemisphere some 12,500 years ago known as the 'Younger Dryas Event'. Whether or not there was such a presence, Britain was certainly inhabited by human beings a short time after the end of the Younger Dryas Event when temperatures once again rose. With the resultant melting of more and more ice, land masses in the northern hemisphere that had previously been pressed down under the weight of ice sheets began to rise. As they did, so too did the surrounding sea levels. These two processes went on in tandem, until, at some point during the co-called *Mesolithic* or *Middle Stone Age*, around 8,000 years ago, the remaining isthmus that had previously connected Britain with continental Europe was finally submerged or breached under the pressure of the rising sea level. Something similar was to happen a little later to the land that had previously connected Britain with Ireland.

By the time Britain and Ireland finally became the islands we know them as today, both had become inhabited by what is estimated to have been a combined total of several thousand stone-age hunters and gatherers who lived in small bands of between 50 and 300 members. Their each becoming an island did not end their further early human settlement, as many of their parts were now easier to reach directly by sea than they had been when they could only be reached from Europe on foot. Throughout the remainder of the Mesolithic period, Britain and Ireland continued to be settled by hunter-gatherer populations, journeying by sea from various different parts of the European mainland on crudely made vessels.

The way of life of these Stone Age settlers in Britain was to undergo a radical change some 6,000 years ago, around 3,900 BC. It did so with the arrival of techniques of farming. The cultivation of crops and the domestication and the raising of animals for food had first been developed in the Near East around 10,000 BC. From there, they had gradually spread northwards and westwards, partly by the migration of whole communities that engaged in them, and partly by their adoption by former hunter-gatherer communities.

Farming considerably increases the yield in food of populations beyond what they could procure for themselves as hunter-gatherers. Farming also makes available to them kinds of foodstuff that enable the mothers of young children to wean them much earlier than they can when consuming the diet of a hunter-gatherer population. Because women are unable to conceive during the period in which they are breast-feeding their off-spring, the adoption of a pastoral and agricultural form of life releases former hunter-gatherer populations from a previously operative natural check upon their birth rates, caused by the much longer lactation periods needed by their infants. The epochal change caused to human society by the development and diffusion of farming has come to be known as the *Neolithic Revolution*. It marked a great step forward in the development of humankind, ushering in a period known as the *Neolithic* or *New Stone Age*.

At one time, it was widely supposed that the Middle Eastern populations among whom farming was first devised and adopted simply spread out geographically as their size grew, thereby coming to displace older and less numerous hunter-gatherer populations. Such a form of mass migration is no longer widely thought to be how farming came to spread into northern Europe generally and Britain in particular. Recent advances in the new and rapidly burgeoning field of genetic archaeology have revolutionised scholarly opinion about early migration patterns within Europe. Rather than Mesolithic hunter-gatherers having been displaced by migrating populations of farmers, it is now more widely supposed that the new agricultural techniques made their way into Britain and northern Europe more generally, if not everywhere else, without much, if any, displacement of their previously resident populations. Thus, as the archaeologist David Miles writes in *The Tribes of Britain*:

> A lot of archaeological evidence suggest[s] that hunter-gatherers in Britain, Scandinavia and north-west France adopted agricultural practices rather than [became] replaced by immigrants... [Thus, seemingly] most Neolithic farmers in Europe were the descendants of Mesolithic hunter-gatherers. Farming and domestication had been passed on as an idea, rather than being brought by waves of new people... [Therefore,] on present genetic evidence it seems that ... the majority of the population in Britain ... can trace its ancestry back into Ice Age hunters...[1]

The advances in genetic understanding that have led to this revision in scholarly opinion arise from greater knowledge that has recently been gained about two distinct varieties of human DNA. One is the Y chromosome, peculiar to males and, therefore, inherited only through the paternal line. The other is mitochondrial DNA or mtDNA for short. This variety of DNA is contained within mitochondria. Mitochondria are structures present in the cytoplasm of all cells essentially responsible for their respiration, and so are possessed by both men and women. Mitochondrial DNA is, inherited only through the maternal line from the mito-chondria contained in the ova of mothers. At conception, the only DNA that male sperm supplies to an ovum is nuclear DNA, which, if it contains the Y chromosome, results in the conception of what will be a boy. Both varieties of DNA periodically undergo small 'random' mutations, but so seldom that each tends to be transmitted in almost wholly unchanged form from one generation to the next. Know-ledge of the similarities and differences in the various mutations of these two varieties of DNA, as found by means of sampling different populations resident in different localities, combined with the recently acquired ability to extract mtDNA from prehistoric skeletal remains, has led to a new science of 'genetic archaeology'. It seeks to combine such knowledge about the prevalence of different mutant forms of these two varieties of DNA as found in different regions with reasonably confident judgements that can be made as to which of them would, at various different times in the past, have been habitable and which not. On the basis of this data, genetic archaeology seeks to arrive at reasoned conjectures as to what possible pattern of human migration in the past best accounts for the present distribution of the various different mutant varieties of these two forms of DNA as found by sampling current populations.

A foremost pioneer of this new field is Bryan Sykes, professor of genetics at the University of Oxford. Together with a team of colleagues, Sykes has carried out extensive surveys of the varieties of DNA found in the inhabitants of various different parts of Europe and Britain. On the basis of the results of these surveys, he has arrived at several evidence-based conclusions about the likely migration patterns in the past that account for their present populations. One of these conclusions, based on the DNA samples of nearly 1,000 people living in different parts of mainland Europe, is that 'the ancestors of most Europeans were hunter-gatherers and not, as was commonly believed ..., farmers who had spread into Europe from the Middle East about 8,500 years ago'.[2] A similar sampling of the DNA taken from thousands of British residents, plus the mtDNA recovered from the teeth of prehistoric human skeletons discovered in the Cheddar Gorge, has also led Sykes to arrive at a similar conclusion in the case of Britain. At the end of 2006, Sykes published the results of his researches in a book entitled *Blood of the Isles: Exploring the genetic roots of our tribal history*. In the final chapter of the book, he summarised the conclusions to which his DNA samplings has led him so:

> I see no reason at all... why many of our maternal lineages should not go right back through the millennia to the very first Palaeolithic and Mesolithic settlers who reached our islands around 10,000 years ago... well before the arrival of farming... [As regards] the change from hunter-gatherers to agriculture... [t]here is no archaeological evidence of conflict and no reason to suppose that the arrival of farmers would have been confrontational... I think the main body of the Neolithics arrived by [a]... western route [along the Atlantic seaboard north from Iberia]... After that, the genetic bedrock on the maternal side was in place. By about 6,000 years ago, the pattern was set for the rest of the history of the Isles and very little has disturbed it since... Overall, the genetic structure of the Isles [suggests] descent from people who were here before the Romans... We are an ancient people, and though the Isles have been the target of invasion ever since Julius Caesar first stepped on

to the shingle shores of Kent, these have barely scratched the topsoil of our deep-rooted ancestry.[3]

Almost simultaneously with Sykes' book on the subject a second book was also published in 2006 entitled *The Origins of the British: a Genetic Detective Story*. Its author, Stephen Oppenheimer, reached strikingly similar conclusions to Sykes concerning how early on it was that most of the ancestors of most of the present-day inhabitants of Britain arrived there. Oppenheimer summarises his conclusions thus:

> The most important message of my genetic story is that three-quarters of British ancestors arrived long before the first farmers. This applies to 88 per cent of Irish, 81 per cent of Welsh, 79 per cent of Cornish, 70 per cent of the people of Scotland and its associated islands and 68 per cent (over two-thirds) of the English and their politically associated islands. These figures dwarf any perception of Celtic or Anglo-Saxon ethnicity based on concepts of more recent, massive invasions. There were later invasions, and less violent immigrations; each left a genetic signal, but no individual event contributed even a tenth of our modern genetic mix... As to who and what were the main British ancestors, we can say they were largely Ice Age hunting families from Spain, Portugal and the south of France.[4]

If it is from such 'immigrants' that most of Britain's past and present population descend, then it is a country of immigrants and descendants of immigrants of remarkably long-standing. Indeed, so long ago did most of the ancestors of most of the present-day inhabitants of Britain appear to have first arrived there that it seems altogether misleading to describe these early first settlers in Britain as 'immigrants' at all. For, as observed earlier, when someone is called an immigrant today, it is implied that they have moved from elsewhere to a place that is already inhabited by a settled population who form an organised society. It is, therefore, equally misleading to describe as being descendants of immigrants to Britain those of its inhabitants who have descended from its very earliest settlers and from whom, it appears, the majority of Britain's present-day inhabitants descend.

By calculating the number of man-hours that would have had to go into the construction of the various megalithic communal burial sites and other Neolithic monuments of which the remains lie scattered about the British country-side, archaeologists have been able to arrive at rough estimates as to the likely size of Britain's population at these remote times. Whereas Britain's hunter-gatherer population is thought to have numbered only between 2,750 and 5,000, one thousand years later, in the early Neolithic period, some six thousand years ago, it has been estimated that the combined population of Britain and Ireland stood at about 140,000, Ireland contributing several tens of thousands to that figure.[5]

In Britain, the Neolithic Age was to last for a couple of thousand years. It was brought to an end some four thousand years ago, when bronze came to replace flint in the making of tools and weaponry. Britain was fortunate in having been prodigiously supplied by nature with both tin and copper from whose fusion bronze is made. The period during which this alloy was used in making tools and weapons is known as the *Bronze Age*. It is thought to have lasted some fifteen hundred years, from between 2,500 BC and 1,000 BC. It ended when bronze was replaced by iron in the manufacture of these implements, a change that initiated the so-called *Iron Age* which lasted some thousand years in Britain. It ended with the arrival of the Romans at the start of the Common Era, not because they introduced some new metal into the manufacturing process of tools and weaponry, for they long continued to be made from iron. The arrival of the Romans brought the Iron Age in Britain to an end, simply because they brought with them the arts of making and keeping written historical records of events. It was the arrival to Britain's shores of such practices that put an end to its pre-history and brought the country into historical time proper.

By calculating the likely number of man-hours that would have been needed to construct the various pre-historic monuments built there at different times, the field archaeologist Frances Pryor has arrived at estimates of the likely size of Britain's population in both the Bronze Age and the Iron Age. During the early Bronze Age, around 2,000 BC, he estimates that Britain's population would most likely have stood at about a quarter of a million.[6] At the end of the Bronze Age a thousand years later, he estimates the population had almost doubled to half a million.[7] He claims there is little archaeological evidence of any significant population increase by the time of the early Iron Age around 700-500 BC. However, there is evidence of such an increase during the Middle Iron Age from 500 BC onwards. The archaeological evidence suggests, he claims, that the increase was not caused by any substantial net inward migration to Britain. It was rather what demographers call a *natural increase*.[8] By this term is meant a population increase in some group over a period due to an increase in the number of live births over the number of deaths.

Until quite recently, the scholarly consensus was that, during the fifth and fourth centuries BC, Britain had been subject to a succession of waves of invasions by a people known as Celts and who were thought to have been distinct and different in ethnicity from its extant inhabitants. That view has increasingly fallen out of scholarly favour. Sceptics have pointed out that the native inhabitants of Britain whom the Romans encountered upon their first arrival would not have referred to themselves as Celts, and nor would these

Romans, This is despite the latter having long been familiar with the term 'Keltoi', it being a word used by the Greeks of the sixth century BC to refer to a group inhabiting a region north of the Alps with whom they then had dealings. In the absence of any traces of such wholesale migrations to Britain during the Iron Age, modern archaeologists now doubt any such Celtic invasions of Britain took place during pre-historic times. As the Iron Age and Roman archaeologist of Britain, Simon James, has put it:

> The major message of the archaeology of the Iron Age is not one of continental connection, but of *local continuity from the preceding Bronze Age*. Mass Celtic invasion into Britain is now implausible. Archaeology in Ireland does not fit with the idea of invasions [there either]... The early peoples of the [British] archipelago, then, were overwhelmingly of local Bronze Age origin, not invaders from the continental homeland of the 'real' Celts... The whole idea of Celts in the islands, and their arrival by migration and invasion from the continent ... is a modern construction, not supported by archaeological evidence.[9]

At the time of the Roman Conquest, it is estimated, the population of Britain stood at somewhere in the region of between one million and one-and-a-half million. That makes its size comparable to that of England's population at the time of the compilation of the Domesday Book some thousand years later.[10] Given that the thousand-year-long Iron Age period in Britain had been one of relative stability, it is less surprising that Britain's population should have trebled in size during that time than that it should seemingly have failed to increase by much in the millennium following the arrival of the Romans. Its apparent failure to grow much during this thousand year period is especially puzzling, given that, during it, Britain underwent several substantial, and historically very important, waves of immigration. They began with the arrival of the Romans and continued with several other later migration waves from northern Europe that followed the withdrawal of the Roman forces in 410 AD. What factors are likely to have prevented Britain's population from growing much during the thousand years following the arrival of the Romans, and how its demographic composition altered during this time, are the matters to which we now turn.

4

From the Roman Conquest to the Norman Conquest

In 43 AD, the Roman Emperor Claudius invaded Britain along with an occupying army of some 40,000 troops. He came on the time-honoured pretext of foreign invaders—namely, having been invited by a local ruler to assist in putting down a local revolt against his rule. The local ruler supposedly responsible for having invited Claudius into Britain was the exiled king of one of its southerly tribes known as the Atrebates. This exiled king, named 'Verica', had supposedly called on Claudius to assist him defeat those of his tribe who exiled him after a palace coup. This supposed invitation to Claudius was to result in a four-hundred-year-long Roman occupation of Britain. During it, the parts of the country most firmly under Roman control were to undergo a huge cultural, but not so huge demo-graphic, transformation.

The Romans named their province *Brittania*, after the name of one the several indigenous tribes whom they there encountered there, the *Brythoni*. They had received their Celtic name from the Gauls, perhaps, on account of their having worn war-paint or some other forms of skin decoration, the Celtic word *pretani* being thought to have meant 'painted people'. Few of the forces Claudius brought with him and stationed in Britain were themselves of Roman extraction. They were mostly of stock that was much more closely related, both genetically and culturally, to the Britons over whom they had come to rule. Most had originated from a part of Gaul that Julius Caesar named *Gallia Belgica* and that now lies within present-day Belgium and Holland.

These Gallic troops had quickly assimilated themselves culturally to the Romans after their own homelands were conquered and subdued by them. Having done so, they would have viewed with disdain the indigenous Britons whom they had been brought over to rule. In time, many of these Britons also came to adopt Roman ways and serve within the Roman regime as 'Roman citizens'. However, during the entire period in which Roman garrisons were stationed in Britain, the number of Roman citizens who had come to Britain from Rome or anywhere else within the Roman Empire only ever formed a small proportion of Britain's overall population. Based on aerial surveys and other archaeological data, it has been estimated that, during the Roman occupation of Britain, the total population of the country stood at somewhere between 2.5 million and 3.5 million. Of these, no more than between at most 100,000 and 200,000 are thought to have been 'soldiers, administrators, merchants and craftsmen from the rest of the empire'.[1] The remainder, who comprised the vast majority of Britain's population, 'were natives whose ancestors had lived in Britain for millennia'.[2]

It was only the southern part of Britain, plus, eventually, Wales that the Romans succeeded in subduing. The tribes which inhabited what we now call Scotland and Ireland always remained outside the sphere of Roman control, even if, initially at least, the Romans were able to contain them. As the centuries of Roman rule wore on, however, all parts of the Roman Empire, including Britain, became increasingly subject to incursion from invaders who came from increasingly more remote regions. Eventually, in 410, Rome felt obliged to recall its garrisons from Britain to deploy them in what turned out to be a vain attempt to stave off barbarian invasion of Rome itself.

During its period of Roman occupation, the parts of Britain that had formed the Roman province of Britannia had grown very affluent, comparatively speaking. They therefore had become an increasingly attractive target for inhabitants of comparatively less affluent regions, after Roman troops withdrew from the province. Even before they had done, and as early as the second half of the fourth century, parts of Britannia had suffered increasingly bold predatory incursions by members of tribes from Scotland and Ireland. It was supposedly on the invitation of native Britons to assist in helping them stave off such marauders from Scotland and Ireland that, in the mid-fifth century, the first of several contingents of Saxons and Jutes arrived in Britain who have collectively become known to posterity as the *Anglo-Saxons*.

The first Anglo-Saxons who settled in Britain did so in the south east and west of the country. At first, they established independent pockets of settlement, living alongside the native Britons among whom they settled. Eventually, the newcomers were to forge for themselves several petty kingdoms out of whose merger in the ninth century there was to emerge Britain's first genuine state— England. The merger of these Saxons kingdoms came about in consequence of their felt need to coordinate defence against a new wave of invaders whose predatory incursions had by then become endemic as well as highly destructive. These were the so-called *Vikings* from Denmark and Norway. It was out of a similar felt need to coordinate defence against this very same enemy that, during the ninth century too, Kenneth MacAlpin had fused the kingdoms of the Picts and the Dalriadans into a single unified kingdom that became known as *Scotia* or Scotland. It did so because the latter of the two tribes from whose merger Scotland had been formed had migrated there from Ireland, and the term

Scotti had been the name the Romans had given to all the inhabitants of Brittania who had migrated there from Ireland.

England or *Angla-land* was named after the Angles. These were an Anglo-Saxon group who had settled in southern Britain during the period between the departure of the Romans and the arrival of the Vikings. It was not only the entire kingdom in the south of Britain to which the Angles gave their name. It also became the name of the language that eventually came to be spoken by its inhabitants, despite the Germanic dialect from which it evolved having been brought to Britain by Saxons, rather than by the Angles.

At first, the Anglo-Saxons appear to have lived alongside the Romanised Britons in separate enclaves. In time, however, these relative newcomers became the dominant cultural and political presence in the land. Their customs and language became the established ones wherever they settled. How the Anglo-Saxons managed to achieve such cultural dominance in England has been the subject of much recent scholarly debate. According to one school of thought that subscribes to the so-called *mass migration model*, the Saxons simply displaced the older populace of Britons in the course of the two succeeding centuries following their arrival in the fifth century. They supposedly did this by a process of ethnic-cleansing that combined slaughter of the indigenous Britons with their westwards migration. They supposedly left the fertile low-lying regions of the south and east of Britain where the Anglo-Saxons increasingly chose to settle, and moved to the more rugged and less easily cultivated environs of Wales and the west country. These latter regions, being less well suited to the forms of agriculture practised by the newcomers, were of less appeal to them. According to those favouring the mass migration model, as many as 200,000 Saxons may have settled in

Britain. Some who support this view claim that the Saxons replaced the Britons, less by slaughtering them than by simply by out-breeding them. Since Saxon law forbade Saxon women from marrying Britons, and since the Saxons tended to be more affluent than the Britons alongside whom they settled, Saxon men were simply able to sire many more children than male Britons.[3]

The main rival school of thought to that which favours the mass migration model to account for how Anglo-Saxon culture became the dominant culture of the south of Britain favours instead what is called the *dominant elite model*. According to those who favour this model, the Anglo-Saxons never did come to replace ancient Britons, either by killing them or out-breeding them. Instead, they maintain, in time Britons simply came to adopt the customs and language of their more affluent and culturally advanced Anglo-Saxon neighbours with whom they eventually became fully assimilated. According to those who subscribe to this school of thought, as few as 10,000 and 25,000 Anglo-Saxons may have settled in Britain during the fifth and seventh centuries. There is currently no consensus on the matter, but David Miles would appear to speak for many when he summarises the current state of scholarly opinion as follows:

> On present evidence it seems that Germanic warriors did attack Britain and then migrate and begin to settle, some with families while others intermarried with the British... The most likely scenario is that ... [t]he Romano-British aristocracy recruited German muscle to support their faltering society. Over some fifty years the opportunities for these bodyguards and raiding war bands became more transparent: whole families and communities shipped out from their Continental homelands... seeing opportunities in a new land... [T]he British in the east and south ... [were probably not] swept away by ethnic cleansing. It is far more likely that they were absorbed into the newly developing English communities... In the course of the seventh century Anglo-Saxon

culture became completely dominant in the lowlands, though genetically perhaps two thirds of the population were of British descent.[4]

Anglo-Saxon culture became the dominant culture within the southern half of Britain during the seventh century. By then, this part of Britain had become divided up into seven weak Saxon kingdoms, each of which had been formed from the previous merger of still smaller kingdoms established by the Saxons there. These seven Saxon kingdoms were: East Anglia, Sussex, Essex, Wessex, Kent, Mercia and Northumbria. It was through their eventual amalgamation in the course of the ninth and tenth centuries that England eventually came into being as a single unified state. Only after that was anywhere in Britain sufficiently well organised and unified, politically and culturally, to qualify for being considered a state and for its inhabitants to qualify as a nation. A unified state of a kind was created in Scotland during the ninth century. However, the ethnic differences between the inhabitants of the two kingdoms from whose merger the kingdom of Scotland was formed meant it lacked the cultural unity that England possessed. Consequently, in the ninth and tenth centuries, it is only England which can be regarded as having become a state and to contain a unified nation. By then, the Welsh had developed a strong sense of their own distinct collective identity, but they never matched it with any real political unity or political organisation until these were imposed on them by the English. In any case, the mountainous terrain of Wales did not attract much foreign settlement to it, and so spared Wales from much immigration until comparatively recent times.

The several Saxon kingdoms from whose union England was formed began their process of confederation in the ninth century. They did so out of their felt need to coordinate defence against the Danes who no longer were content with mere spoils from their predatory raids as they had formerly been. Instead, from early on in the ninth century, Danes had begun to overrun and settle in Britain. They managed to carve out for themselves an extensive area of north east England, located above an imaginary line between London and Chester, known as the 'Danelaw', within which their authority held sway from the late ninth until the eleventh century. The genetic similarity between Saxons, Danes, and Normans makes it practically impossible on the basis of genetic evidence alone to distinguish between their respective descendants. However, Saxons and Danes are both thought to have made a significant contribution to Britain's demography, especially in certain parts of the country. Bryan Sykes estimates that roughly '10 per cent of men now living in the south of England are the patrilineal descendants of Saxons or Danes, while above the Danelaw line the proportion increases to 15 per cent overall, reaching 20 per cent in East Anglia.'[5]

The Saxon kingdom that was most instrumental in the creation of England as both state and nation was Wessex. It came to assume this role in the latter part of the ninth century during the reign of King Alfred. By this time Wessex was the only Saxon kingdom that had not been overrun by Danes. As well as temporarily managing to repel a Viking invasion of his kingdom, Alfred succeeded in absorbing and integrating within it such Vikings as by then had chosen to settle there. During the comparatively long ensuing period of peace and stability he was able to win for his kingdom against the Danes, Alfred laid down within it both the necessary institutional and cultural foundations for England's subsequent creation as a single unified and unitary state. This was something, however, that only began in the following century during the reign of Alfred's son, Edward the Elder, and that of his grandson, Athelstan, and was subsequently developed much further by the Normans and Angevins.

The institutional foundations of England that were laid down during the reign of Alfred are several. They include the many fortified towns or burghs he was instrumental in creating during his reign, as well as the more uniform and unified administrative and judicial system he introduced through codifying its law in the vernacular and by requiring the inhabitants of its boroughs and rural shires periodically to assemble to implement that law on pain of fine. So far as concerns his contribution to creating a unified English culture, Alfred was instrumental in the creation of a national vernacular English literature within the southern half of Britain. He achieved this by initiating and vigorously supporting an extensive programme of translation into the vernacular of such national-consciousness-raising texts as Bede's *Ecclesiastical History of the English People*, as well as by instigating a literacy programme designed to maximise familiarity with this literature by the inhabitants of his kingdom.

It was, however, not Alfred but his grandson Athelstan who was the first king of Wessex to be crowned also king of the English. By then, all that was further needed before the emergence of England as a unitary state was complete was the incorporation of Northumberland. This was accomplished during the reign of Alfred's great grandson, Edgar.

England, however, was still highly vulnerable as a state even after then. It might easily have become absorbed, both culturally and politically, within some Scandinavian confederation. That this never happened was, arguably, as much the result of fortune than of anyone's design. Edgar's son was the hapless Ethelred the 'Unready'. To ingratiate himself with the Normans and thereby win their support,

Ethelred married a daughter of Richard I, Duke of Normandy, named Emma. She bore him the son, Edward, who eventually succeeded him as king of England. Known as 'the Confessor' on account of his piety, this king Edward died in 1066 by which time Normandy had fallen under the rule of William, a grandson of its former Duke, Richard I. Despite his marriage to a daughter of the Earl of Wessex, Edward the Confessor died without heir. Supposedly, on his deathbed, he had nominated his brother-in-law Harold to succeed him. But this king Harold was not allowed to reign for a day without having to face challenge for his crown from rival claimants one of whom was William, Duke of Normandy.

William based his claim to the English throne upon his assertion that, some years earlier, Harold had sworn fealty to him as overlord, after being shipwrecked off the coast of Normandy and falling captive to William, a version of events that Harold always denied. William, however, succeeded in persuading the Pope of his version of events who himself was less than happy with the degree of independence from his ecclesiastical authority that the church in England had lately been showing, and who therefore had reasons of his own for wanting a form of regime-change there that would bring its church closer to Rome. William managed to persuade the Pope to decree that, in refusing to acknowledge and honour his oath of fealty to William, Harold had forfeited his title to the English throne. On that basis, William declared all the nobility and churchmen in England who sided with Harold and against him to be traitors who thereby had forfeited their title to whatever lands they formerly had held in England. Armed with the pope's support for divesting his opponents in England of all their lands, William set sail for England in September 1066. He came with an armada of between four hundred and six hundred ships on which he brought with him some 10,000 troops, largely but not exclusively of French extraction. There were also Bretons and Flemings among those who had enlisted with William in the hope thereby of eventually acquiring land in England or other forms of reward for helping him gain the English Crown.

After defeating Harold on the day of his arrival in a battle at Hastings at which not only Harold but two of his brothers also fell, William pressed on to London, putting to the sword all who stood in his way. He arrived there at the beginning of December in time to receive the crown of England on Christmas Day in the newly completed Norman abbey at Westminster, the construction of which Edward the Confessor had made his life's work. After his coronation, William pressed on to the north and then to the west of the country, ruthlessly putting down all opposition, often in the most brutal manner imaginable. Given how violent was the manner by which William gained the lands in England that he divided up between himself and his most senior aides, the title 'bloody foreigners' as applied to them seems not entirely inappropriate.

5

From the Norman Conquest to the Reformation

As was pointed out earlier, when considering how much of a nation of immigrants Britain can truly be considered to be, it is not helpful, indeed it is positively misleading, to count as immigrants to it all who settled there before the Norman Conquest. This is because, as used today, the term 'immigrant' tends to be reserved only for those who move from elsewhere to somewhere that is already inhabited by a people among whom there have grown up sufficient mutual affinities, relations, and bonds to qualify them for being considered a nation, and enough political organisation and unity as qualifies their territory as a state.

This was certainly the view espoused by the economic historian William Cunningham in his classic study *Alien Immigrants to England*, published in 1897. Cunningham, however, began that work by making an observation that superficially suggests he held the opposite view of the matter to that which has just been ascribed to him. He wrote:

> So many diverse tribes and stocks have contributed to the formation of the English nation that it is not easy to draw a line between the native and the foreign elements... It seems a little arbitrary to fix on any definite date and designate the immigrants of the earlier times, component parts of the English race, while we speak of the later arrivals as aliens.[1]

After giving due consideration of the matter, however, Cunningham eventually decides 'to take the reign of Edward the Confessor as the starting-point, and to treat the Normans as the first of the great waves of alien immigration into England'.[2] His stated reason for so doing is that:

> When we speak of aliens and foreigners, our language implies the existence of political institutions and settled life...We cannot properly speak of the 'far-coming man' as an alien, till... national life was to some extent organised.[3]

By this token, of course, as Cunningham himself recognises, the first foreigners to settle in Britain who, strictly speaking, should be considered as immigrants to it are the Danes who settled there during the reign of King Alfred. Cunningham, however, does not choose to consider them so. Instead, he prefers to regard them in the same way as, he informs the reader, the Normans regarded them, namely, 'as merely that English tribe which effected the latest settlement in Britain'.[4] Either way, so small was their overall number relative to the number of those already in Britain when they arrived that, even if we were to treat the Danes and not the Normans as the country's first true immigrants, their settlement still did not do much to make Britain very much more of a nation of immigrants than it had been before they arrived. Nor, for similar reasons, did the arrival of the Normans and all who followed in their immediate wake, all of whom can and should be regarded as immigrants. For again, comparatively speaking, their numbers were only very small. As has been observed of them:

> Unlike their Angle, Saxon and Viking predecessors, the Normans did not come *en masse* and settle the land... [O]nly ten thousand or so Frenchmen followed in William's footsteps – less than one per cent of the population... But they were the *crème de la crème*... When William died in 1087, one-third of the kingdom was owned by just 180 immigrant lords. And of the sixteen bishoprics in the land, only one was held by a non-Norman.[5]

The total number of Normans who settled in England is estimated never to have comprised more than five per cent of its total population.[6] However, while theirs numbers were comparatively small, their impact on the country was enormous and long-lasting, not least upon its physical appearance. Not only was William quick to reinforce his temporal rule by building numerous stone castles across the country, but the Norman churchmen who soon followed him were no less eager to reinforce their spiritual authority there by constructing cathedrals, abbeys and numerous stone churches.

The Norman Conquest, however, was much more than a simple land-grab and a change in the personnel comprising England's ruling elite, although it was certainly both these things among many others. As has been noted: 'within five or six generations—by the end of the reign of Henry II in 1189—England, if not Britain, had a quite new political, military, commercial and religious establishment'.[7] The changes England underwent as a result of the Conquest went much beyond these. Hardly any aspect of life was unaffected by the settlers.

In addition to the various political, military and religious changes William made to the structure and organisation of English society, primarily to consolidate his hold over the country, he also made several commercial and economic innovations no less profound or long-lasting. To finance his military campaign, as well as reward those who had helped him gain the country, William was in need of liquid funds. They were needed, not least to pay those who had supplied him with the fleet on which he had transported his invading army to England. To obtain these funds, William turned for credit to several Jewish financiers resident in Normandy. These were members of an ethnic minority in Europe who had already begun to acquire a degree of expertise and acumen in the field of finance, so many other avenues of endeavour having being officially closed off to them. Along with his soldiers, William brought over a small number of these Jewish financiers. They initially took up residence in

London, subsequently being joined there by spouses and children. Later, these Jewish financiers and their families, together with others from Normandy, spread throughout England, establishing small communities in nearly every major commercial centre. Even so, their overall numbers were small, amounting to no more than an estimated total of between 5,000 and 6,000.[8]

Until they were expelled from the country at the end of the thirteenth century, the Jews who settled in England in the wake of the Norman Conquest fell there under the direct protection of the king, not that of any local magnate. As well as financing royal activities, they began in time to extend credit to several other prominent figures, among whom were several Norman bishops, the construction of whose cathedrals in England Jewish capital helped to finance. Initially, these Jewish immigrants from Normandy enjoyed friendly relations with the king, church, and nobility. However, their relations with others in England started to deteriorate soon after the beginning of the thirteenth century, after some Anglo-Norman nobles, including Simon de Montfort, had become heavily indebted to and hence resentful of them. A succession of ever-more cash-hungry English kings found their Jewish subjects becoming less able to pay the ever more exorbitant special taxes that these kings were wont to impose on them. Relations between Jew and gentile became further strained in England during that century by several edicts promulgated by successive Lateran Councils of which one required all Jews domiciled anywhere within Christendom to wear distinguishing insignia on their apparel to make their ethnic identity apparent to all. Additionally, stories began to circulate in England, occasionally provoking minor pogroms there, that Jews practised periodic ritual slaughter of gentile children to procure blood for use in Jewish ritual foodstuffs. Such stories did little to enhance their popularity among the local population. Edward I made a half-hearted attempt to regularise their settlement by opening other trades up to them besides money-lending, after his father Henry had forbidden Jews from engaging in it. This attempt to regularise the settlement of the Jews in England was always destined to fail, since the opportunities for work in England offered to them remained hide-bound and severely restricted. By the time it became clear to Edward that his attempt at regularising their settlement in England had failed, the Jews there had become so impoverished as to be of little further use to the Exchequer. Accordingly, in 1290, they were summarily ordered to leave the country. While the thirteenth century historian Matthew Parris claimed that as many as 16,000 Jews left England in that year as a result of the order, more recent scholars estimate their number at the time of their leaving to have been no more than between two and four thousand.[9]

The expulsion of the Jews from England in 1290, however, did not end the practice of usury there, any more than it had ever been a monopoly preserve of Jews in medieval Europe in the first place. By the time the Jews were forced to leave England, its economy had become so thoroughly commercialised it could not possibly have survived without a fresh supply of moneylenders to fill the financial vacuum created by their departure. The financial shoes left vacant by the expulsion of the Jews were quickly filled by bankers and financiers from Lombardy. Traces of their settlement survive in such place-names as Lombard Street in the City of London, as well as in the names of England's pre-decimal currency, such as the florin and the acronym 'Lsd', composed from the first letters of the three Italian words that designated each of its three principal denominations: *lire,* pounds; *soldari,* shillings; and *dina,* pence.

Jewish and Lombardian financiers were not the only economic immigrants whom William and later Angevin kings encouraged to settle in England. As Robert Winder has pointed out:

> The Normans were keen to see England's towns settled by Frenchmen, to prevent the formation of any revolting Saxon strongholds; but immigrants from elsewhere were also encouraged, by the granting of mercantile privileges, to put down roots. Foreigners were preferable to Saxon merchants, as their main interest was clearly commercial rather than political. It was easy for newcomers to obtain royal permits to engage in trade.[10]

In the centuries that followed the Norman Conquest, many French Cistercian monks also came over to England, establishing monasteries which began to farm sheep for wool on an industrial scale. Initially, in order to be woven into cloth, the wool these monasteries produced had to be shipped abroad, for until then weaving had been confined in England exclusively to the natural economy of the household, almost all of the output of which was put to domestic use, rather than sold. However, in Flanders weaving had long been carried out on a commercial basis, and it was not long before Norman rulers persuaded Flemish weavers to settle in England and practice their craft there. From the twelfth century onwards, this was something many of them started to do. They settled in such Norfolk towns as North Walsham and Worstead. The name of this latter town became that of the cloth Flemish weavers started to produce there which it retained even after its manufacture relocated to the Midlands. In time, such woollen cloth became the principal export of England and its main earner of foreign currency, especially in Elizabethan times. Its large-scale production on a commercial basis was not the only contribution made by the economic immigrants who settled in the wake of the Norman Conquest. German and Dutch beer brewers also settled, the Dutch ones introducing the cultivation of hops into Kent for use in brewing.

Despite all the foreign immigration to Britain resulting from the Norman Conquest, it was still by no means a country of immigrants. Some two centuries after the Conquest, when England's population stood at somewhere between four and four-and-a-half million, which was double what it had been at the time of the Conquest, most Englishmen and women were still 'ethnically English—that is Anglo-Scandinavian and British stock—rather than Norman-French'.[11]

By the beginning of the fourteenth century, England's population could not have been less than 5,500,000 and may have been as large as 6,500,000.[12] Within half a century, however, it had fallen drastically as a result of the arrival to its shores of a most unwelcome new visitor. This was the 'Black Death', the plague which first reached the south coast of England in 1348 and swiftly spread throughout Britain. It quickly reduced its population by a third and it remained low for the next century-and-a-half. It has been estimated that, in the early part of the sixteenth century, Britain's population was not much above half of what it had been at the start of the fourteenth century. 'The population... of England, Wales and Scotland numbered no more than three million... in the later fourteenth century, half the level it was in 1300. By the early 1520s it was scarcely higher.' [13] Part of the reason Britain's population failed to grow for over a hundred and fifty years following the Black Death of 1381 was a recurrence of outbreaks of similar diseases. It also appears, however, that, during this time, many people there simply became increasingly reluctant to marry, or at least to have children, perhaps, understandably, fearing the worst for them. This failure of the country's population to grow much during this period remains something of a puzzle, given that, because of the comparative scarcity of labour, real wages had become relatively high. Britain's population, however, did begin to stage a recovery early in the sixteenth century:

> From 1525 the demographic brakes were at last released, and the stagnant British population accelerated into rapid growth. Within fifteen years there were an additional half-a-million English people—an increase of about a quarter... By the end of the sixteenth century... the English population [had] reached four million and the Welsh had grown from approximately 210,000 in 1500 to 380,000 in 1603.[14]

This sudden spurt of population growth during the Elizabethan period, however, was not sustained for long into the seventeenth century. Until 1750, population growth in Britain remained very slow, as Andrew Hinde observes in his recent demographic history of England:

> Population growth rates in England during this period were modest. From about 2.7 million in 1541 the population grew steadily throughout the rest of the sixteenth century to reach about four million by 1600. Although growth continued into the seventeenth century, it petered out during the 1650s and the population stagnated from then until after 1700. After that it resumed, though rates were modest, so that the best estimate we have of the population of England in 1750 is about 5.7 million, which is probably less than the total around 1300.[15]

After 1750, Britain did experience rapid and continuous population growth until the Second World War. At first, this growth in population was only comparatively modest in size, but it accelerated steadily. The result was, according to Hinde, that: 'the number of inhabitants ... increased to eight million by 1794, ten million by 1812 and 15 million in the early 1840s. In other words, during the period 1750-1850 the population of England increased to a level more than double its previous highest value.'[16]

Despite, being augmented from early on in the sixteenth century by a steady stream of immigrants, from then on until the Second World War very little of Britain's net increase in population can be attributed to immigration. Virtually all of its increase was a purely natural one. As J.A. Tannahill observed in a book published not long after the end of that war:

> Britain is not by tradition a country of immigration. In fact, between 1815 and 1914, she not only quadrupled her population without resorting to large-scale foreign immigration, but also despatched over 20 million people to destinations beyond Europe, at first largely to the USA and later in ever increasing proportion to the developing countries of the Commonwealth.[17]

How much immigration to Britain occurred between the sixteenth century and World War Two, where its immigrants came from during this period, and with what impact on Britain's overall population, are the matters to which we now turn.

6

From the Reformation
to the Second World War

Wales and Scotland form parts of Britain every bit as
integral to it as England. Therefore, in considering how far
Britain may be said to be a nation of immigrants, it is
necessary to consider how much immigration each of them
has received from places other than different parts of Britain.
Enormously important as each undoubtedly has been to
Britain's history, and equally as important as has been
Ireland with which Britain was united politically between
1801 and 1922, inward immigration into all three of these
countries from places other than elsewhere within Britain
has contributed little to the size of Britain's population. This
is so for several reasons.

In the first place, the respective populations of Wales,
Scotland and Ireland have only ever comprised a small
proportion of Britain's total population in comparison with
that of England. This can be seen from Table 6.1 that shows
the size of their respective populations in millions between
1750 and 1911:

Table 6.1

	1750	1801	1851	1901	1911
England	(5.7)				34.0
		9.1	18.0	32.6	
Wales	(0.6)				2.0
Scotland	(1.2)	1.6	2.9	4.5	4.8
Ireland	(3.0)	5.2	6.5	4.4	4.4
UK-total	(10.5)	15.9	27.4	41.5	45.2

Source: Davies, N., *The Isles: A History*, London: Papermac, 2000, p. 651.

Secondly, until comparatively recently, little foreign immigration into Britain has come about through foreign settlement in Wales, Scotland, or Ireland. Most foreign immigrants have always chosen to settle in England. In the case of neither Scotland, nor Wales, nor Ulster, can the majority of their respective inhabitants, therefore, rightly be considered to be immigrants to Britain or descendants of immigrants to Britain. Instead, as with England, the majority of their inhabitants have been British-born, descended from ancestors the first of whom settled in Britain, in the majority of their cases, before any of the states and principalities had come into existence from whose union Great Britain has been formed as a state. So, the vast majority of Welsh, Scots and Northern Irish can no more be said to descend from ancestors who acquired citizenship of Britain by immigrating there than can the majority of Englishmen and women.

The majority of Ulster's present–day population might well descend from ancestors who first settled there only after it had become a province of England. However, the vast majority of these ancestors of present-day Ulstermen and Ulsterwomen first settled there in the sixteenth and seventeenth centuries. Moreover, they came to Ulster either from England or Scotland. So, despite having settled in Ulster from elsewhere, they can hardly count as immigrants to Britain, even if, for present demographic purposes, Ulster is treated as a part of Britain. Nor were the majority of these sixteenth and seventeenth century settlers in Ulster themselves descendants of immigrants to Britain. This is because, in the vast majority of their cases, their ancestors would have been resident in Britain since before any part of it had become a state or part of one, and hence before any settlers in Britain who had come from elsewhere can rightly be considered immigrants to Britain.

Between the start of the sixteenth century and the end of World War Two, of far greater size than all other foreign immigration streams to Britain has been that from across the Irish Sea. Most immigration to Britain from Ireland took place in the decades following the Irish potato famine of 1846. Those who came from there were motivated to do so by dire economic need. In the twenty-year period between 1841 and 1861, the number of Irish-born adults living in Britain more than doubled, rising from just below 300,000 to over 600,000. By the 1880s, the Irish expatriate community in Britain is estimated to have stood at more than a million, forming over three per cent of Britain's total population.[1] This is a significant proportion, but hardly one that can be said to have turned Britain into a nation of immigrants. In any case, at the time Ireland was in full political union with Britain. So, in a sense, those Irish who settled in Britain then may not rightly be thought of as having been foreign immigrants, nor their descendants, therefore, thought of as descendants of immigrants to Britain. Rather, they were internal migrants within the United Kingdom. Nevertheless, for present purposes, the Irish who then settled in Britain will be treated as immigrants to Britain and their descendants who remained there considered as descendants of immigrants to Britain. This is because they certainly considered themselves of distinct nationality from the British, and the British reciprocated those feelings in full. Large as the wave of immigration to Britain from Ireland has been, both up to the Second World War and even subsequently, it has never accounted for more than three per cent of Britain's overall population at any given time.

In comparison with that from Ireland, all other varieties of immigration to Britain between the sixteenth century and the end of World War Two have been small, both in number and as a proportion of Britain's total population. Even when aggregated together, their combined total nowhere approaches the number of Irish who immigrated into Britain during that same period. Thus, given that Irish immigration accounts for at most only three per cent of Britain's population, the other forms of immigration to Britain during this period can hardly be said to succeeded in turning it into much more of a nation of immigrants and descendants of immigrants than it had been at the start of the sixteenth century when, as we have seen, it most decidedly was not. By briefly considering in turn all the other principal immigration streams to Britain besides that from Ireland between the sixteenth century and World War Two, we shall see how little Britain's demography was changed by them.

Between the sixteenth century and World War Two, besides those who came from Ireland, Britain was the terminus of two other principal streams of immigration. In some ways, each of these is more striking than that from Ireland, despite being smaller in size. While Irish immigrants came to Britain from motives similar to those which had prompted all previous immigrants to Britain— namely, a desire to better their economic circumstances— those who came as part of these two other immigration streams were motivated otherwise, at least initially so in the case of one of them. Both, therefore, constitute novel historical phenomena. Since the end of World War Two, each of these immigration streams has outgrown in size that which still continues to flow from Ireland, but even in their smaller pre-War incarnation, each has considerable historical importance in its own right.

These two other principal streams of immigration to Britain besides that from Ireland each came about as a result of a different event of world-historic significance that took place at the start of the early modern period. The first such event was the opening up of the world resulting from the series of great pioneering voyages made at the very end of the fifteenth century under the sponsorship of Spain and Portugal by Christopher Columbus and Vasco da Gama. These led to the 'discovery' not only of the Americas but also of a sea route from Europe to the Far East around the cape of Africa. As a result of their discovery, Europeans were brought for the first time into contact with the native inhabitants of the newly discovered Americas in which the Spanish were quick to plant colonies. They were also brought into much closer contact than ever before with the inhabitants of Africa and the Far East, continents long known to them but which were now much more easily reached and which were likewise subject to colonisation, in the first instance by the Portuguese.

In the case of Africa, many of its native inhabitants were soon to find themselves victims of a massive form of involuntary trans-world migration of great historical import that was to issue in a small amount of incidental immigration to Britain. These involuntary African 'migrants' were victims of the trans-Atlantic slave-trade that began to operate from Africa's west coast after it became opened up to European navigators. The first European countries to engage in such trans-Atlantic slave trafficking were the same pair as had been the first to undertake the great voyages of early modernity, namely Spain and Portugal. It was not long, however, before England, followed suit. In 1497, Henry VII sponsored the Venetian John Cabot to undertake a voyage across the Atlantic in quest of a north-west passage to the Far East. Although no such passage was discovered— not surprisingly since none exists—Cabot's voyage did result in the 'discovery' of Newfoundland and New England, territories that England was to claim for itself. It was through its claim on the second of these territories that

England secured a toehold in the North American continent that was to prove so fateful in the succeeding centuries.

The first immigrants to Britain who came as a result of these great sea voyages of early modernity, however, did not come from these newly discovered North American territories, despite a brief visit to London in 1616 by the native American 'princess' Pocahontas. They had begun to come well over half a century before her, and their point of embarkation was not any part of the newly-discovered Americas, but Africa. Nor did they come from any colonies England had established within that continent, for they started to arrive well before any had been established there by England. The first Africans to immigrate to Britain were brought there by Scottish and English adventurers who had taken them as bounty from Portuguese ships they had captured off the African coast from where Portuguese slave-traffickers had purchased them from African slave-traders. Not long after their arrival, other African slaves started to arrive. Some were brought by their owners to learn English better to assist them in breaking into the lucrative transatlantic African slave-trading market that had sprung up within the Spanish empire in the Americas. The following quotation provides an illuminating summary account of the less than altogether happy circumstances in which the first African immigrants arrived in Britain:

> A small group of Africans were recorded at the court of James IV of Scotland in the early 1500s... probably... taken from a Portuguese slave ship by... Scottish privateers acting with the King's permission... By the summer of 1555, a group of five black Africans [had] arrived in England from the coast of what is now Ghana, [so as to learn] English to help open the way into the closed Portuguese West Africa trade in slaves, gold, ivory and pepper... [T]he first [Englishman to enter] into the trans-Atlantic slave trade... [was] John Hawkyns who... in 1562 bought slaves from African merchants, stole more from Portuguese slavers and

kidnapped others... [H]e carried 300 people from the Guinea coast to Hispaniola... and exchanged them for... [local produce].[2]

Soon after John Hawkyns' first pioneering venture into the slave trade, there began to arrive in Britain a small steady trickle of African slaves. Their number started to grow considerably from the mid-seventeenth century onwards, after Oliver Cromwell acquired Jamaica and English ships began bringing African slaves there to work on its sugar plantations. This stream of African immigrants was to dry up towards the end of the eighteenth century, when slavery and the trade in slaves began to become widely abhorrent to British sensibilities. Before then, it has been estimated, no fewer than 10,000 mostly male African slaves were brought to England to work there in that capacity or else as domestic servants.[3] Few, however, are thought to have had any children, so their contribution to Britain's population would not have been great which is not to say it was nothing. A recent article[4] in the *European Journal of Human Genetics* reports that seven white British males, who share a rare surname derived from a village in East Yorkshire but who are apparently unrelated, have the same rare type of Y chromosome that is seldom found outside West Africa where it is typical. None of these men were aware of having any African ancestors, but their family genealogies were traced back to two eighteenth century Yorkshire families. This suggested they had a common West African male ancestor in the early eighteenth century, who probably arrived in Britain as a slave, although the possibility that he was a north African Roman soldier who came to Britain eighteen hundred years earlier has not been excluded. Such cases, however, remain very rare indeed. A survey of the Y chromosomes of 1,772 British men failed to find any of similar type to that most frequently found among African men, contrary to expectation had there been a substantial pre-War immigration to Britain from Africa.

Nor, until after the end of World War Two, was Britain's population very much augmented by immigrants from the Far East, a second group of immigrants who came there as a result of the voyages of discovery of early modernity. Most of these initial Far Eastern immigrants to Britain came there in one or other of two capacities. If male, they came as *lascars*; if female, as *ayahs*. The former were crew-members of ships of the British mercantile fleet who had been taken on in India or China and then laid off after their ships had arrived in British ports. Some of the more enterprising of these 'marooned' *lascars* began to open and run in their ports of arrival boarding-houses and dining-halls catering for fellow *lascars* which would later become the nuclei of subsequent pockets of settlement by Far Eastern immigrants after the War.

The *ayahs* who settled were nannies to the small children of British *nabobs*, the relatively high-up administrators of the East India Company, returning home along with their families and other Indian servants. Originally, the East India Company had simply operated as a trading company, after it had been granted a monopoly license to trade in the Far East by Elizabeth I. It was, however, during the reign of Charles II that the company acquired its first territorial foothold in the Indian sub-continent. This took the form of the trading outpost of Bombay that Charles had received as part of the dowry that accompanied his Portuguese bride, Princess Catherine of Braganza. Finding the cost of its upkeep too great, Charles made over this trading outpost to the East India Company in return for a modest annual rental. The company grew in size and influence enormously from the mid-eighteenth century onwards which was when the *ayahs* and other Indian personal servants of its returning employees began to arrive in Britain in considerable number.

Although much is sometimes made of the presence in Britain of these *lascars* and *ayahs,* overall they contributed little to the country's demographic composition, since their numbers were only ever very small. Roger Ballard, Director of Manchester University's Centre for Applied South Asian Studies, has summarised their demographic impact as follows:

> Until the beginning of the twentieth century the South Asian presence in Britain remained minute. At any given time it would have included no more than few hundred Ayahs and Lascars, [and] a rather smaller number of students seeking professional qualifications, whilst the number of princes and other aristocrats — most of whom only made the briefest of visits — could probably have been counted on the fingers of one hand.[5]

In addition to the various small streams of immigration that began to flow to Britain from Africa and the Far East from early on in the early modern period, there also started to flow into Britain from this time on a second entirely different stream of immigrants of no less historical importance. This was the by-product of a second momentous event at the beginning of the early modern period. This second great event was the Reformation, that great fissure within Christendom at the beginning of the sixteenth century that split Europe into a northern Protestant half and a southern half that remained staunchly Catholic. It took a couple of very bloody centuries before the various different Christian denominations of Europe managed to work out a *modus vivendi* to enable them to live in peace with each other, despite their religious differences. Until then, much blood was spilt in Europe as a result of Christian fighting Christian on account of doctrinal difference. It was such inter-denominational conflict that precipitated, apart from immigration from Ireland, the second principal stream of immigration to Britain besides that from Africa and the Far East. What occasioned it was the need of the immigrants who composed it to flee their homelands to escape persecution for their religious convictions.

It may have been Henry VIII who initiated the Reformation in England, but it was his daughter Elizabeth who consolidated that break from Rome. Neither monarch, however, could guarantee its irreversibility beyond their own respective lifetimes. This was something that was only achieved gradually during the course of the succeeding century. To remain Protestant, the country had to undergo a bitter civil war, regicide and a further bloodless Revolution at the end of the seventeenth century.

Neither Henry nor Elizabeth remotely qualify for being considered tolerant in matters of religion. Yet one consequence of their break from Rome was to make England a haven for persecuted Protestants coming from throughout Europe from the sixteenth century onwards. England continued to remain one during the Stuart dynasty of the succeeding century and well into the early part of the eighteenth century. Thereafter, the internecine warfare sparked off by the Reformation and Counter Reformation had abated sufficiently to end the need for this kind of immigration, at least for a considerable time. While these intense religious conflicts raged, the population of England was periodically subject to augmentation by the arrival there of intermittent waves of religious refugees coming from different parts of Europe in quest of asylum. Their impact on the country's subsequent economic development was out of all proportion to their comparatively small number.

The first and most sizeable group of such religious refugees to settle in England were the French-speaking Calvinists from France and Flanders who have become collectively known as the *Huguenots*. They began to arrive as early as 1562, often without any intention of remaining permanently, although many subsequently did. It was only ten years later, however, following the St Bartholomew's Day Massacre in 1572, that they started to come in any large number. In a matter of days, 2,500 Huguenots were slaughtered in Paris and no fewer than 10,000 Huguenots were killed before this episode ended. At the end of the sixteenth century, as a result of the promulgation in 1598 of the Edict of Nantes, Huguenots gained a century's respite from the most brutal forms of their persecution, but its revocation by Louis XIV in 1685 opened the floodgates to a second large wave of persecution of them that in turn served to trigger a second and much larger wave of immigration to England. The overall number of Huguenots who settled in England is estimated to have been somewhere between 40,000 and 50,000, making up as much as one per cent of its then overall population.[6] England's Huguenot émigré community was a remarkably accomplished and a comparatively affluent one. Not only did they bring with them industrial and commercial skills, they also brought considerable wealth of which the country was then badly in need and from which it greatly benefited.

The Huguenots initially settled just outside of the City of London in the district of Spitalfields. It still continues to bear testimony to their former presence, both in many of its street-names, such as Fashion Street and 'Petticoat' Lane, named after their principal trade of silk-weaving, as well as in the fine town houses still standing in such streets as Fournier Street built to accommodate their families and the silk-weaving workshops they installed in their upper storeys. Introducing into England silk-weaving, hat making, and the use of jewels in watch-making, considerably improving the accuracy of their time-keeping, the

Huguenots also brought with them considerable liquid capital that they quickly placed at the disposal of the wider host community, to very good effect from its point of view. As Robin Gwynn has explained in his book *The Huguenot Heritage*:

> England was faced in the 1690s by a war burden that was massive by comparison with the nation's past experience and existing taxation ...Wars raged between 1689 and 1713 (with a precarious peace between 1697 and 1702)... The experience of the past century – [plus] the state of near-bankruptcy brought about by the second and third Anglo-Dutch wars – augured ill for England's chances of survival. That she not only survived but conquered was in large part due to the ... 'financial revolution' [of the 1690s], which witnessed the birth of a new world of banks, of stocks and shares, of new credit instruments and public debt... This transformation was significantly assisted by the refugees – especially those based in the City and the east London suburbs.[7]

As well as French Huguenots, England also became a sanctuary during the sixteenth and seventeenth centuries to several other groups of religious refugees who came there to escape religious persecution at home. Of these, the most numerous group were Calvinists and Lutherans from the Low Countries whose various Germanic dialects led the English refer to them all indifferently as 'Dutch'. These 'Dutch' religious refugees began to arrive from the mid-sixteenth century onwards, after Charles V of Spain, who combined with the throne of Spain the office of Holy Roman Emperor, imported into the Dutch imperial provinces the techniques of Inquisition for rooting out heresy which had first been devised and perfected within his Spanish kingdom. Upon his abdication in 1556, Charles divided up between his two sons his two domains. He preserved Spain's rule of Holland by detaching it from the Empire of which it had formerly been part and giving it to his son Phillip upon whom he also bestowed the Spanish throne. A short while after, in 1581, the largely Calvinist Dutch populace broke from Spanish rule to become a fledgling republic.

Although these 'Dutch' religious refugees were immensely talented and influential, their numbers settling in England were comparatively small. They remained such even after 1688, when, following the 'abdication' of its openly Catholic king James II, Parliament invited William of Orange to assume the vacant throne in consort with his wife, Mary, the Protestant daughter of James. The glorious, because bloodless, revolution in England of 1688 finally ended all prospect of England's future re-Catholicisation. It did so, partly, by Parliament legitimising its transfer of the throne to a Protestant line by the pretence of construing the flight of James to France as abdication. It also did so partly through the enactment of the Exclusion Act of 1701 prohibiting a Catholic from ascending the English throne in the future. The matter was sealed in 1707 when England entered into full political union with Scotland which before then had been a fully independent state with its own king and parliament. England's motive for entering into union with Scotland was to eliminate the possibility that any future Stuart claimant to the English throne might be able to gain a bridgehead there from which to pursue a claim to the English throne with the aid and backing of Catholic France with which England continued to remain at odds throughout the eighteenth century. The 'price' the Scots were able to extract from the English for agreeing to give up their own parliament and ruling dynasty was free access for the first time to England's by then not inconsiderable and rapidly burgeoning overseas dominions, both for purposes of trade and settlement. The Scots were also allowed to keep their own national church, educational and judicial systems, and were given very generous representation in the

Westminster Parliament. These terms of union were ones with which, until recently, virtually all Scots have been seemingly happy, save for a few Highlanders.

As well as the various French and 'Dutch' Protestant refugees who settled in England during the early modern period to escape religious persecution, the Reformation was indirectly responsible for the settlement in England in the mid-seventeenth century of another of Europe's persecuted religious minorities, but one whose persecution had not been triggered by the Reformation. These were Jews who returned to England after an official period of absence there of some 350 years. The Reformation was implicated in their return since it was negotiated during the Protectorate of Oliver Cromwell. His strong Puritan beliefs had convinced him of the truth of the biblical prophecy that foretold the Messiah would not return before the Jews, for their sins, had been scattered to all four corners of the earth. By effecting their readmission, Cromwell allowed himself to be persuaded that he was helping to expedite the Second Coming. Another decidedly more this-worldly consideration that may well have weighed more heavily with Cromwell was their wide dispersal across Europe. This made the Jews a potentially valuable source of reliable foreign intelligence, as well as a conduit by which safely to convey intelligence abroad in pursuit of the imperial ambitions which Cromwell increasingly began to harbour.

Initially, no more than a score of Jews returned to England, in the first instance all from the fledgling Dutch Republic to which their ancestors had fled from Spain and Portugal a century or so earlier to escape the Inquisition. The Jews who immigrated to England from Holland in the mid-seventeenth century came after they had begun to doubt the ability of the Dutch republic to withstand the forces of the Counter-Reformation. Like the Huguenots before them, and as so many other subsequent immigrants to England have since done, initially they gravitated to London's East End. Their number was initially only very small and remained small during the eighteenth century, despite the arrival during it of several thousand German Jews. According to James Walvin, historian of immigration to Britain, 6,000 Jews were resident in Britain in 1734, and only 5,000 some twenty years later.[8] By the beginning of the nineteenth century, estimates of the number resident vary between 20,000 and 30,000.[9]

At that point in time, the flow of *religious* refugees coming to Britain dried up and did not resume until towards the end of the nineteenth century. However, the ensuing period of relative tranquillity that Europe enjoyed during the eighteenth century proved only short-lived. Before that century was out, Britain once again found itself becoming a sanctuary to a new species of European refugee—the political émigré. Such refugees started to arrive there from France as early as 1789 to escape the excesses of the Revolution that had just broken out. By 1792, it is estimated no fewer than 40,000 such émigrés had crossed the English Channel to take sanctuary in England.[10]

It was the arrival of these French émigrés, and not that of Eastern European Jews towards the end of the nineteenth century, that led Parliament in 1793 to enact the first piece of legislation in modern times designed to control the entry of foreigners. This was the Aliens Act. It was enacted, less to curb the entry of genuine French émigrés, for whom there was considerable sympathy in Britain, than to safeguard against the possibility of the country being infiltrated by a fifth column of French radicals masquerading as political refugees. This emergency measure introduced to the statute-book many forms of immigration control that have since become commonplace. They include the need for aliens to be able to give good cause before being granted entry, their need to register upon arrival by signing a declaration at their entry ports, and the possibility of their deportation. One casualty of the Act was Talleyrand who was obliged by it to leave Britain for America.

Upon termination of hostilities between France and Britain in 1815, the 1793 Act fell into desuetude, and was replaced in 1836 by another Aliens Act offering a much lighter regulatory touch, although it still required aliens and the ship-masters conveying them to the country to register their arrival. For the greater part of the nineteenth century, however, Britain was to pride itself on the asylum it was willing to grant those fleeing from their home-land to escape persecution on account of their beliefs. Among the most notable of such political émigrés who took advantage of the sanctuary it provided were Giuseppe Mazzini and Karl Marx. Overall, however, the number of such political refugees who settled in Britain during the nineteenth century was very small.

In addition to the French émigrés who came to Britain at the beginning of the nineteenth century, the French Revolution was also indirectly responsible for what proved to be the largest stream of inward migration into Britain during that century—namely, that from Ireland. Just as, at the beginning of the eighteenth century, England had entered into political union with Scotland so as to neutralise a threat it might otherwise have posed by possibly becoming the jumping-off point for a French invasion of England, similarly, at the start of the following century, Britain entered into a corresponding full political union with Ireland in order to neutralise the threat it might otherwise pose by becoming a base from which Napoleon could launch an invasion. It was because of this union that Irish nationals became able to enter Britain freely throughout the nineteenth century. Ireland's political union with Britain created the anomalous situation of its affairs being decided at Westminster by a parliament from which most Irish were denied any form of representation on account of their Roman Catholic faith. Growing awareness of how untenable such an anomaly was led to the enactment in 1828 of the Catholic Emancipation Act, which, in turn, made inevitable the extension of the franchise effected by the Reform Act of 1832. Catholic emancipation also paved the way for Britain's Jews beginning to be accorded full political rights, the most affluent and well established ones becoming able to vote and assume public office, including as MPs, from the mid-nineteenth century onwards.

However, as the century wore on, the steadily brightening prospects of Anglo-Jewry became increasingly shrouded by the arrival in England of increasing numbers of impoverished Jews from Poland and Russia, especially from the early 1880s. Many were seeking to escape the mounting wave of pogroms that had broken out in these countries following the assassination of Czar Nicholas II in March 1881. By 1880, the number of Jews in Britain is thought to have been about 65,000. A huge tidal wave of migration of Eastern European and Russian Jews, without historical precedent, was then to sweep the planet. Part of it was to end up in Britain. Between 1880 and 1914, it is estimated that almost three million Jews left Eastern Europe and Russia. The majority of these ended up in the United States. However, 150,000 of them are estimated to have settled in Britain.[11] In the ten-year period between 1891 and 1901, 59,000 Jews arrived and a further 67,000 followed over the next five years.

After years of Parliamentary debate, the British authorities eventually responded to this large influx of poor Eastern European Jewish immigrants by enacting an Aliens

Act in 1905. This piece of legislation introduced onto Britain's statute book for the first time a number of fairly stringent immigration controls: '[It] established an immigration control bureaucracy with powers of exclusion and enabled courts to recommend "undesirable aliens" for deportation... [and] created controls over the movement of aliens and obliged them to register with the police.'[12] Although among the Act's supporters were undoubtedly some principally motivated by anti-Semitism, the curbs it was designed to place on the settlement of Jewish immigrants were introduced less on account of their religion than of their destitution which the authorities feared, should they be admitted, would leave them without any recourse but to criminal activity. By means of the Act, the British authorities reserved for themselves a right to refuse entry to all aliens judged to be 'undesirables'. Some have claimed the act far too draconian and brutal a measure, but some take a different view. For example, David Coleman observes of it: 'The act was a modest measure. It only enabled the newly appointed Immigration Officers to identify and refuse entry to aliens among the steerage passengers of larger vessels who were deemed to be "undesirables". Decisions were subject to appeal.'[13] Although the Act left undefined who was to be considered an 'undesirable', only prospective immigrants who had travelled in steerage on boats carrying more than 25 passengers were subject to consideration for entry. And of these, only those with criminal records or judged unable to support themselves and their dependents were liable to be refused entry. Even then, entry was not denied to those who had been victims of religious or political persecution.

As well as alarming the British authorities, the arrival in Britain of large numbers of destitute Jews from Eastern Europe filled their co-religionists already domiciled there with equal foreboding. They feared that, unless the new arrivals could quickly be found accommodation and employment and speedily integrated, all without placing any strain on the public purse, their arrival might trigger a wave of anti-Semitism in Britain similar to that from which they were fleeing that might also engulf those Jews already in Britain. Responsibility for the welfare of their newly arrived and impoverished co-religionists fell to the Board of Guardians for the Relief of the Jewish Poor, created in 1859. Mounting tensions between it and the Whitechapel local authority over the squalid and increasingly in-sanitary living conditions of the new arrivals led to the creation by the Board in 1885 of an East End Enquiry Commission under the chairmanship of Nathan Mayer Rothschild, shortly to become Britain's first Jewish peer. Among the recommendations of the Commission was the urgent need for the Anglicisation of the new arrivals. As the Commission stated in its report, 'steps must be taken to cause the foreign poor upon arrival to imbibe notions proper to civilised life in this country'.[14]

The Anglo-Jewish community responded swiftly to the challenge posed by the arrival of their co-religionists. They quickly provided accommodation and jobs for them. They also laid on education for their children to ensure their prompt and full integration. Most of the newly arriving Jews came through the Port of London, settling in the same streets and houses of London's East End as the Huguenots had formerly lived in. Given current concerns about social cohesion and the potential obstacle that special faith schools of their own pose for the full integration of some of Britain's more recently arrived religious minorities, it is worth noting the large and positive role that Jewish faith-schools played at that time in integrating the children of newly arrived Jewish immigrants:

Schools... were the main vehicles for integration... The Jews' Free School in Bell Lane led the way... Between 1880 and 1914, one third of all London's Jewish children passed through its doors. Many were foreign born, and arrived unable to speak English. The school taught them English from day one, provided them with a refuge and a means of escape from poverty, educated them in both secular and religious studies, anglicized them and sent them out in the world fit to integrate into society... The *Jewish Chronicle* boasted that a young Pole could be placed in the Jews' Free School with the assurance that at the end of his training he would be turned out a young Englishman.[15]

Whether or not it was because of its enactment, soon after the 1905 Aliens Act became law, Jewish immigration to Britain fell away. In the eleven succeeding years, fewer than 30,000 additional Jews were to settle in Britain. However genuine a threat to public safety their immigration may have seemed to the British authorities, its scale was nothing like as great as that which resulted from the successive waves of equally as impoverished and uneducated Irish immigrants who began to arrive in Britain from the mid-nineteenth century onwards: 'The number of Jewish settlers, in little over a quarter of a century, was 155,811. When we compare this with the Irish figures (the number of Irish-born living in England in 1891, 1901, and 1911 were 458,315, 426,565 and 375,325 respectively) it is clear that the Jews came nowhere near the level of Irish immigration.'[16]

Indeed, from the beginning of the sixteenth century, until World War Two, neither the immigration stream flowing to Britain from Africa, nor that from Asia, were as great as that from Ireland. Nor was the volume of immigration to Britain from Ireland during this period matched by such immigration there as came about as a result of the arrival of successive waves of religious and political refugees during it. Neither severally, nor together, was the number of immigrants to Britain from these several other streams as great as the number of Irish immigrants who settled in Britain during this period. Moreover, and more importantly for our purposes, none of these various pre-War immigration streams to Britain, including that from Ireland, had much impact on Britain's overall demographic composition because of the very substantial natural increase it underwent during this same period, especially after 1830. That natural increase meant that, notwithstanding a huge amount of *emigration* from Britain during this period up to the end of World War Two, largely to its dominions like Australia and Canada and also to the USA, immigration to Britain never added any more than a few percentage points to its population. To repeat J.A. Tannahill's telling observation quoted earlier: 'Britain is not by tradition a country of immigration. In fact, between 1815 and 1914, she not only quadrupled her population without resorting to large-scale foreign immigration, but also despatched over 20 million people to destinations beyond Europe.'[17]

Whilst the scale of pre-War immigration to Britain was highly limited, nonetheless the tumultuous events of the first half of the twentieth century resulted in several forms of foreign immigration to Britain during its first four decades that, after the war, were to prove of great historical consequence so far as immigration is concerned. When hostilities between Britain and Germany broke out in 1914, the mother country quickly sought assistance from her large overseas dominions in its war-effort. Such assistance was not long in coming. During that war, as many as two-and-a-half million British colonials fought on Britain's behalf, and many thousands more helped in a civilian capacity, filling vacancies in British factories and the mercantile fleet created by the enlistment of British citizens in the armed forces. Upon cessation of hostilities in 1918, the returning British servicemen expected and did receive preferential treatment over these colonials. In the summer of 1919, anti-black riots took place in Cardiff, Newcastle, Liverpool and London. Despite being nominally British subjects, the Africans and West Indians who had come to Britain from her colonies during the war were treated by the British authorities as though they were aliens. Thus, as all aliens had been required to do since the outbreak of hostilities in 1914, they too were required to register their presence with the local police, as well as being liable for deportation, if judged undesirable. In 1931, indignation at what he perceived to be the unfair treatment by Britain of its African and West Indian colonial subjects led a Jamaican doctor settled in Britain to create there a campaigning organisation called the 'League of Coloured People'. This organisation, together with other pan-African organisations created in Britain during the inter-war period by a small elite of African university students there, helped to awaken in Britain's African colonies a desire for independence that was to bear fruit of varying degrees of sweetness after the end of World War Two.

In addition to the African colonials who came to Britain as a result of the First World War, there was also considerable recruitment of *lascars* into its mercantile fleet who had come to make up a quarter of its crew members by the end of the war.[18] Upon termination of hostilities, several thousand of them, resident in British ports, were laid off so that their employers might accommodate returning British ex-servicemen.[19] Some found work in British factories and, during the inter-war period, were joined by a number of better-off and more highly educated Indians. No fewer than 1,000 Indian doctors took up medical practice in Britain during this period.[20] The overall number of immigrants from the Indian sub-continent who settled in Britain during the inter-war period, however, was only ever very small comparatively speaking. It never exceeded 6,000 to 7,000 in all.[21] Their importance, however, far exceeded their numbers, since they often became the nuclei around which later immigrants from south Asia would constellate after 1945.

Because of Ireland's close historic links with Britain, immigrants from there remained able to enter Britain freely even after its secession from Britain in 1922. This was two years after Britain had imposed immigration restrictions that required foreign aliens seeking entry for purposes of work to have obtained beforehand a work permit from the Department of Employment for which only their prospective employers could apply, and also despite Ireland's neutrality during World War Two. As a result of such freedom of entry, Ireland continued to be the single biggest source of immigration to Britain even after it gained independence from Britain. Next to Irish immigrants, the next single largest group to settle in Britain during the inter-war period was some 60,000, typically well educated and relatively affluent, Jewish refugees from Nazi Germany, among the most notable of whom were Sigmund Freud and Nicholas Pevsner. Between the resumption of hostilities between Britain and Germany in 1939 and their termination in 1945, only a further 10,000 Jews managed to find sanctuary in Britain of whom many spent a good part of the war interned in the Isle of Man. Many tens of thousands of other European refugees did succeed in gaining entry to Britain after 1939, however, including some 20,000 Poles.[22] In addition to various European refugees who became domiciled in Britain, during the war, it became once again the temporary home to several thousand British colonials from the West Indies, Africa, and the Indian sub-continent. They had come there with the active encouragement of the

British authorities to fill vacancies in munitions and chemical factories, as well as serve in the mercantile fleet.

None of these multiple streams of immigration to Britain occasioned by the Second World War had the effect of turning the country into any more of a nation of immigrants than it had been before it, when it most certainly was not one. For example, the entire South Asian presence in Britain is estimated to have exceeded no more than 'a few thousand'.[23] However, unknowingly at the time, those whom the war brought to Britain from overseas were preparing the ground for a large wave of immigration from many of Britain's former colonies who began to arrive there not long after hostilities ceased in 1945. The demographic significance for Britain of the war has been well summarised by James Walvin thus:

> Between 1939 and 1945 Britain experienced the most remarkable and large-scale migration of peoples in its history. It was as if Britain had been rapidly converted into a giant transit camp... The result was that Britain in wartime became a fascinating mix of nationalities and races... The war ... exposed many West Indians and Africans to social experiences and the wider world which would ... break down the old colonial system... Indeed, one major consequence of the war was that Britain began to receive the settlements of alien people and colonial citizens on a scale and at a pace which had never previously been experienced. It was of course impossible to realize it at the time, but the war was ultimately responsible for many of the demographic changes which took place in Britain in the post-war years.[24]

7

From the Second World War
to the Present

Since the end of World War Two, Britain has undergone immigration on a scale never previously experienced. To gain some idea of just how comparatively recent and vast in scale the increase in the size of immigration to Britain has been over the last 60 years, especially in the last decade, consider the following demographic statistics from the Office of National Statistics:

- *In 2001, 4.9 million (8.3 per cent) of the total population of the UK [had been] born overseas ... more than double the 2.1 million (4.2 per cent) in 1951. The increase in ... the foreign-born population between 1991 and 2002 was ... nearly 1.1 million, greater than in any of the preceding post-war decades... While 92 per cent of people born in the UK identified themselves as white in 2001, [only] 53 per cent (2.6 million) of the foreign-born population was white.[1]*

- *Migration into the country increased from 265,000 in 1993 to 513,000 in 2002 ... Over the decade to 2002, 3.9 million people entered the country as migrants... In 2002, and each of the three preceding years, international, migration contributed approximately 80 per cent of the UK's annual population increase.[2]*

- *In the decade [to 2004], migration into the country increased from 314,000 in 1994 to 582,000 in 2004,* **with most of the increase to inflows occurring after 1997**... *Between 1994 and 1997, net inflows of international migrants fell.... The net inflow of 223,000 in 2004 was the highest since the present method of estimation began in 1991.[3]* (emphasis added)

- *In the year to mid-2005, the UK population increased by 375,000 ... the largest annual rise in numbers since 1962... Natural change (the difference between births and deaths) contributed one third of the population increase. Net migration and other changes contributed the other two thirds. Until the mid-1990s, natural change was the main driver of population growth. Net international migration into the UK from abroad is [now] the main factor in population growth.... In the year to mid-2005, an estimated 588,000 people migrated to the UK for a year or more.[4]*

This staggering recent increase in immigration to Britain needs to be viewed in the context of the overall increase of Britain's population during this same period. That increase, in millions and disaggregated by constituent country, is detailed in Table 7.1 (p. 92).

What is striking about these statistics is how geographically confined they show to have been the increase in the size of Britain's population since 1950. Almost all of the country's population growth has occurred within England where the overwhelming majority of Britain's post-war immigrants have chosen to settle. Moreover, and with only very few exceptions, most notably the Chinese, rather than spread evenly throughout England, most of Britain's post-war immigrants have, understandably, chosen to settle only in such places as already had come to contain significant numbers of those from the same places of origin as themselves. In the case of many immigrants, the number of such localities has been very restricted indeed. The result of such a pattern of settlement has been the creation within England over the last half-century of several towns and city districts containing very high concentrations of particular ethnicities, often of only comparative recent settlement. In proportion as this has occurred, so many such towns and districts have increasingly started to turn into self-sufficient minority enclaves whose residents have decreasing need or opportunity to come into contact with and hence adjust their habits and customs to those of the wider community. The scope for social fragmentation has thus increased with the growth of these enclaves.

The self-segregation of some minorities within such enclaves is something that had been remarked on by social commentators as early as the mid-1990s, well before the riots in Bradford and Oldham of 2001, let alone the London tube-bombings of July 2005. For example, in 1996, broadcaster Jeremy Paxman offered the following comment about the massive rise in Britain's Afro-Caribbean and South Asian population that had taken place between 1951 and 1991, during which their combined number increased from 80,000 to three million:

> It is quite an explosion. Furthermore ... immigrants are concentrated in England... and comparatively absent from Scotland Wales... Over two thirds of the entire ethnic minority population of Britain is concentrated in the south-east of England and the West Midlands. Parts of cities like London, Leicester or Birmingham now appear to have no connection with the England of Arthur Bryant. In these areas, multiculturalism is... a fact of life, in which the Church of England has been replaced by mosques or temples and the old corner grocers by *halal* butchers and sari shops. In Spitalfields... 60 per cent of the population is now Bangladeshi. In parts of Bradford, over half the population now comes from Pakistan.[5]

Apart from a huge increase in their overall numbers, little has changed in terms of the concentration of these minorities in the eight years since Paxman made this observation. Over three-quarters of Britain's ethnic minority population were revealed by the 2001 census to be concentrated within London, the West Midlands, and three other areas. Fewer than three in ten of the residents of the London borough of Brent were revealed to be white, and nearly three-quarters of the residents of one Bradford suburb were revealed to be of Pakistani origin. According to the same census, almost a quarter of the population of Dewsbury, a town in west Yorkshire, were found to be of south Asian origin, their number having grown there by 60 per cent during the preceding decade. One of its districts was found to be 90 per cent south Asian. This district is Saville Town of which one former resident was Mohammed Sidique Khan, leader of the July 2005 London tube-bombers and of which it has been recently said that: 'It is possible for a Muslim child to grow up—in the family home, at school and in the mosque and madrassa—without coming into any contact with Western lifestyles, opinions or values.'[6]

Such large concentrations of increasingly segregated ethnic minority populations are growing rapidly. This is because the immigrants settling in them are far below the average age of the population and have comparatively high rates of fertility, reflecting the family patterns of their countries of origin. In 1950, Britain's ethnic minority population formed just over one per cent of the total. By 2001, it had grown to eight per cent and it is continuing to increase fast. Assuming no change in fertility rates or in immigration levels, it has been estimated that, by the end of the present century, Britain will come to contain more non-whites than whites, London being expected to reach this tipping point as early as by the end of the present decade.[7] Based on figures from the 1991 Census, it has also been calculated that, during the decade to 1991, Britain's white population grew by only 0.9 per cent, while its non-white population grew by 42.7 per cent. Furthermore, because of the low fertility rate of Britain's white population, most of the increase in their numbers during that decade was due to immigration from the EU and Eastern Europe.[8] Using these same growth rates, it has been estimated that, should they continue, by 2073, Britain will cease to have a predominantly white population, with England ceasing to somewhat before then. Accordingly, if, in 1945, Britain could not remotely be said to be a nation of immigrants and descendants of immigrants, in light of these forecasts, the country can be said by now to be well on the way towards becoming one.

What could have brought about such a major demographic transformation of the country in such a short space of time is the question to which we now turn. In accounting for this demographic transformation of Britain over the past six decades, when it turned from being an essentially mono-ethnic mono-cultural society into a much more ethnically and culturally diverse one, it will be convenient to divide up the period into four sub-periods. The first such period runs from 1945 to 1948; the second from 1948 to 1971; the third from 1971 until 1997; and the last from 1997 to the present. Immigration during each sub-period will now be considered.

1945-1948

Post-war immigration to Britain today is commonly associated with that originating from former British colonies and, more latterly, from the new accession countries of European Union. In the immediate post-War period, however, it was nationals of some of the very same Eastern European countries from which large numbers of immigrants are presently coming to Britain who first began to settle there. Their settlement is little spoken of today, but at the time their arrival was much discussed. As J.A. Tannahill observed in his 1958 monograph *European Volunteer Workers in Britain*: 'Displaced persons from Europe ... are now well-known figures in many British cities... It is less often realised that their admittance to work in Britain represented a revolution silent and striking, in the official policy of controlling entry to this country.'[9]

Just how much of a silent revolution was the admittance to Britain of these displaced Europeans is indicated by the fact that: 'Whereas in 1939 there had been only about 239,000 aliens over the age of 16 in the United Kingdom (of whom... about 80,000 were refugees) this figure had, by December 1950, been increased to 424,329. The increase of roughly 200,000 was the net gain from the admittance in these years of approximately 250,000 aliens.'[10]

The most sizable group of such immigrants were 130,000 Poles of whom 100,000 had served in the Polish Armed Forces (PAF), all of whom were offered the opportunity to settle permanently in Britain after the war. The remaining 30,000 Poles who settled were dependents of members of the PAF who took up the offer.[11] The next largest such group were displaced Eastern Europeans who, at the end of the war, had ended up in various camps in Europe, labour camps or prisoner of war camps, and who were unwilling to be repatriated to their home countries because they had fallen under Soviet rule. Eighty-five thousand of them were recruited to Britain under various official schemes to meet labour shortages. They included: Estonian, Latvian, and Lithuanian women recruited in German labour camps, under the 'Baltic Cygnet' scheme, to work in British hospitals as nurses and domestics; Ukranian prisoners of war and various others recruited under the 'Westward Ho' scheme to work in industries with labour shortages; and a group of 17,000 nationals of countries against which Britain had fought in the war and who were only temporarily admitted. They comprised 10,000 Sudeten German women, 2,000 Austrian women, and 5,000 Italians of both sexes.[12] Most of this group of 17,000 subsequently returned home.[13]

1948-1971

The start of this second post-war sub-period witnessed the beginning of a wholly novel demographic phenomenon. Initially only very small, but soon becoming very much larger and constantly growing, this was a wave of immigration to Britain from parts of its former empire in the West Indies and the Indian sub-continent. It came about as the result of the combined effect of two factors. The first factor was the highly unpropitious economic conditions in its countries of origin. The second factor was an acute labour shortage in Britain during the latter part of the 1950s which prompted public and private sector employers to recruit directly from these two regions.

New Commonwealth immigration to Britain began shortly after the end of the war, when West Indian troops stationed there during it returned home for demobilisation and found economic conditions there so unpromising that they promptly took advantage of their freedom to enter Britain which, at the time, was still extended to all citizens of British colonies, both those still extant as well as former ones like India and Pakistan which had just gained independence. Such freedom of entry had originally been extended to all inhabitants of the British Empire by the Imperial Act of 1914. The British Nationality Act of 1948, passed in the wake of India's and Pakistan's independence in that same year, similarly extended a right of entry to them all, even after their countries had gained their independence.

West Indians began to arrive in Britain in increasing numbers during the 1950s, often after having been recruited in the West Indies by British public-sector employers, most notably London Transport and the National Health Service. They had been preceded in 1948, however, by the arrival of several hundred Jamaicans who had come to Britain on board the *Empire Windrush*. They had made their pioneering journey without previous recruitment by any British employer, and without the invitation or encouragement, and initially even the knowledge, of the British authorities. In some ways, their migration is owed to the enterprise of the captain of the captured and renamed former Nazi troop-carrier which brought them. During its three day berth in Kingston harbour, to which it had gone to collect and return to Britain from leave 60 West Indian Royal Air Force servicemen, he had hit on a way to fill his three-quarters empty ship by offering passage on it at half-fare. When it docked at Tilbury, few of the 450 West Indian civilian passengers who had been attracted to make the voyage by the cheap fare, and of whom nearly all were young men, had any jobs to go to or anywhere to stay. Temporary accommodation was hastily arranged for those in need of it in a disused underground shelter at Clapham Common. Its close proximity to a Streatham labour exchange accounts for why, to this day, this part of south London is home to such a large Afro-Caribbean community. Their numbers grew quickly from these very small beginnings, approaching 250,000 by 1961; over 400,000 in 1965; and climbing to over half-a-million by 1971.[14]

Unlike Britain's first post-war immigrants from the West Indies, many of those who came from south Asia arrived after previously being recruited by British employers, typically owners of textile mills in the Midlands and Yorkshire, keen to take advantage of this source of cheap labour. Often, their recruitment was made on the basis of their personal recommendation by other south Asian employees at these mills who were the kinsmen or fellow villagers of those recommended and who themselves had been recruited whilst resident in Britain, having worked there during the war in munitions factories or else on board ships belonging to Britain's mercantile fleet that had been torpedoed in the Atlantic. Thus began what has proved to be a very lengthy process of chain-migration.[15] Because of their mode of recruitment, many of Britain's post-war immigrants from south Asia had relatives there with whom to stay upon arrival. As in the case of the West Indian immigrants, the overwhelming majority of those who initially came from south Asia were male. Like their West Indian counter-parts, they had been attracted to Britain by the very much larger incomes that could be earned there and for which they were prepared to work long and unsocial hours, often doing nightshifts. They were also prepared to work for lower wages in jobs that offered less favourable working conditions than those available to the indigenous working population at a time of relative labour scarcity, which meant these immigrants posed no serious economic competition to the indigenous population. Additionally, as a result of their singular mode of recruitment, the post-war immigrants from south Asia also tended to be drawn from a relatively small number of highly specific localities and, correspondingly, liable to settle in a few highly specific localities in Britain where kinsfolk were already present.

Britain's first south Asian immigrants after the war were Punjabi Sikhs from the Jullundur Doab. They tended to settle in such midland towns as Birmingham and Leeds, as well as in the London borough of Southall. Soon after them followed largely Hindu Gujaratis from the Surat district on the coast north of Bombay. They have tended to stick less closely together than the Sikhs, having become more widely dispersed throughout the outer suburbs of London. The next group of immigrants to begin to come to Britain from south Asia were Mirpuris and Cambellpuris from the northeast region of Pakistan who were invariably Muslim. They began to arrive in substantial number in the late fifties after work began on the construction of the Mangla Dam that displaced many Mirpuris. The immigrants from Pakistan have tended to concentrate within highly segregated enclaves in such towns as Bradford and Leeds. They have tended to remain in these towns long after the textile mills in which they initially came to work had closed, without replacement by new alternative sources of employment. This has led to high levels of unemployment in these towns, as well as large concentrations of ethnic minority populations, a particularly volatile mix. The last group of south-Asian immigrants to settle in Britain are Muslim Bengalis from the Sylhet district in the north-east of the Indian sub-continent. Today, this district falls inside the country of Bangladesh which, before 1971, was East Pakistan. The British Bengali community in Britain has tended to concentrate together, especially in Birmingham and the London borough of Tower Hamlets. Many of those who live in Tower Hamlets now live, work, and worship in the same buildings as were formerly used for these same purposes by its Jewish population who, with growing affluence, have long since moved to the suburbs of northwest London.

The post-war immigrants from the Indian sub-continent began to arrive in Britain somewhat later than did those from the West Indies. Hence, despite their rapid growth in numbers during the 1960s, Britain still contained fewer south Asian immigrants than immigrants of Afro-Caribbean extraction in 1970, as shown by the following estimates of their respective numbers (Table 7.2, p. 74).

By the late 1950s, so great had the pace and scale of New Commonwealth immigration into Britain become that, following racially motivated disturbances in Notting Hill in 1958, and with the rate of economic growth in Britain beginning to slow, mounting public concern about deteriorating race relations led to the enactment in 1962 of the Commonwealth Immigrants Act. This piece of legislation was designed to curb the flow of primary immigration from the New Commonwealth. It did so by denying entry to Britain of Commonwealth citizens unless they satisfied one of the following three conditions. They must either, first, hold a British passport, or, second, have previously obtained an employment voucher, or else, third, be a dependent of a British passport-holder or someone who had arrived with an employment voucher or who was already settled in the UK. The requirement that Commonwealth immigrants seeking entry to Britain without a British passport must first obtain a work voucher was similar to, but less specific than, one which, since 1919, had applied to nationals of countries outside the British Empire. They could only enter Britain to work after having obtained a work permit for which only a prospective employer could apply.

Table 7.2
Number of West Indian and South Asian Immigrants
to United Kingdom, 1951-71

	West Indian	Indian	Pakistani	Bangladeshi
1951	28,000	31,000	10,000	2,000
1961	210,000	81,000	25,000	6,000
1971	548,000	375,000	119,000	22,000

Source: Peach, C. (ed.), *Ethnicity in the 1991 Census, Vol. 2: The ethnic minority populations of Great Britain*, London: HMSO, 1991, Table 5, p. 9.

Paradoxically, it has been suggested that the 1962 Commonwealth Immigrants Act may actually have had the opposite of its intended effect of reducing immigration. This is because, prior to its enactment, New Commonwealth immigrants, of whom the overwhelming majority were male, had seemingly been content periodically to return home to visit friends and family to whom they had often been sending money. With the passing of the 1962 Act, immigrants such as these faced the danger that, if they left the country for a home visit, they might be denied re-entry to Britain. The prospect of its imminent enactment led to a last minute rush into the country of New Commonwealth immigrants eager to beat the barrier about to descend. Its enactment thereby precipitated a novel demographic phenomenon of chain-migration. The wives and children of immigrants joined them after the latter had been forced by the imminent prospect of its enactment to choose between taking up permanent domicile in Britain, and bringing over their wives and children to join them, or else returning home permanently. However, it is by no means certain that this form of chain migration would not in time have begun of its own accord even had the 1962 Act never been passed.

The 1962 Act still privileged Commonwealth citizens over non-Commonwealth citizens in terms of entry to the country. For, unlike the latter, the former were able to enter without any prior specific job to go to. All they now needed was a work voucher of which, initially at least, many were made available to those without any special skills. During the 1960s, however, a steadily tightening domestic labour market led to the withdrawal of vouchers for those without any special skills, as well as to steady annual reductions in the number of vouchers allocated for other sorts of work.

Further restrictive legislation was enacted in 1968 as a result of the so-called 'Kenyan Asian' crisis of 1967. This crisis was a consequence of the process of Africanisation whereby African nationals took over key jobs from non-nationals in their newly independent countries. The Kenyan Asian crisis of 1967 was precipitated by President Kenyatta 'inviting' 80,000 Asians resident in Kenya to leave the country. The families of many of these predominantly middle-class south Asians receiving this 'invitation' had originally settled in Kenya before India and Pakistan had been granted independence. As a precaution, many had obtained British passports when they were freely available to all citizens of the British Empire. After President Kenyatta had made plain his wish that they leave the country, many of these Kenyan Asians indicated their intention to enter Britain on the strength of their British passports, rather than return to the Indian sub-continent. The prospect of their imminent arrival led to the enactment in 1968 of a second Commonwealth Immigration Act designed to prevent them doing so. It did this by requiring all Commonwealth citizens who sought to enter to Britain indefinitely without a work voucher to prove a parent or grandparent of theirs had been born in Britain or else had undergone naturalisation there.

A further piece of legislation, enacted in 1969, was designed to tighten still further controls over immigration to Britain from New Commonwealth countries. This was the Commonwealth Appeals Act. It required all prospective immigrants to Britain, who sought entry as a dependent of some settled immigrant, to present upon arrival an entry certificate obtained after personal interview at the British High Commission of their country of departure certifying the authenticity of their claimed relationship to whichever resident in Britain they were claiming to be joining as a dependent.

One final piece of legislation made the immigration status of Commonwealth citizens the same as that of non-Commonwealth citizens. This was the Immigration Act of 1971. It required all seeking entry to Britain without a work-permit for more than a temporary visit to prove their so-called *patriality*. By this term was meant a person's possession of UK citizenship in virtue of satisfying one of the following three conditions: first, having been born, adopted or naturalised in the UK; second, having a parent or grandparent who satisfied one of the former conditions; or, finally, having been accepted for settlement there through having resided in Britain for five years. As before, Irish citizens remained able to enter Britain freely, as they still can do. Until recently, they remained the principal group of immigrants to Britain in the post-War period.

These various pieces of legislation managed to bring primary immigration from New Commonwealth countries firmly under control. However, a steady and not inconsiderable stream of secondary immigration continued to flow into the country from the Indian sub-continent through family reunion and marriage. The latter remains an especially well-used route into Britain among Pakistani immigrants whose families tend to be both large in size and to favour arranged marriages between first cousins.

The countries of Ireland and the New Commonwealth were by no means the only ones from which Britain received immigrants between 1948 and 1971. By the end of this period, there had grown up there a Chinese community of some 50,000 strong, largely originating from Hong Kong. Their numbers had grown from a mere 5,000 in 1951. Similarly, between 1955 and 1960, almost 50,000 Greek Cypriots settled in Britain. Many of them came as a result of the conflict in Cyprus between Cypriots of Greek and Turkish extraction. In 1974, these expatriate Greek-Cypriots were joined by a further 11,000 Turkish Cypriots who came to Britain in wake of disturbances in Cyprus that followed its invasion by Turkey in that same year. Likewise, by 1971, Britain had become home to 100,000 Italian-born economic migrants. Over 40,000 Maltese immigrants also took up residence in Britain between 1959 and 1974.

1971-1997

Despite all these various streams of immigrants to Britain, plus several additional smaller ones, Britain received no disturbingly large further amounts of net immigration between 1971 and the end of the Cold War in 1989. That it did not was the product of two factors. The first was the firm controls over primary immigration from New Commonwealth countries put in place during the 1960s and 1970s. The second factor was the very substantial levels of emigration from Britain to Old Commonwealth countries during this same period.

This situation changed radically at the end of the 1980s when the Iron Curtain was lifted in 1989, symbolised by the destruction of the Berlin Wall in that same year. This event served to trigger Germany's re-unification shortly after, followed by the break-up of Yugoslavia, civil war in Bosnia, and finally the disintegration of the Soviet Union a few years later. Although, at the time, all these momentous events were (with the exception of civil war in Bosnia) unreservedly welcomed by the West, and not without good cause, they turned the 1990s into a decade of marked political instability and conflict throughout the countries of the former Soviet Union and Eastern Europe, as well as those in Africa and the Middle East that had previously been under Soviet influence. The demographic shockwaves sent out by these conflicts were quickly transmitted to the member states of the EU sharing common borders with former Warsaw Pact countries. The form that these shockwaves assumed was a very substantial and sudden increase in the number of refugees and asylum-seekers arriving in these west European countries from various war-torn parts of the Soviet Union's former empire in Eastern Europe, most notably Yugoslavia, as well as from more remote countries that had formerly lay within the Soviet Union's sphere of influence, such as Somalia and Zimbabwe.

It was not long before these same demographic shockwaves reached the shores of Britain. Large numbers of asylum-seekers began to appear in Britain and other west European countries in the early 1990s, mostly coming from various impoverished parts of Eastern Europe, the Middle East and Africa. Many turned out to be disguised economic migrants who had often come with the assistance of organised people-traffickers who, seizing the opportunity presented by Europe's more permeable borders, had quickly turned clandestine entry and bogus asylum-seeking into major growth industries. During the 1980s, no more than about 4,000 asylum-seekers had come to Britain each year.[16] After 1991, their annual number started to rise steeply and quickly, and has since remained comparatively very high. This is despite a reduction in the annual number of applications for asylum to Britain since 1996, a fall in asylum-seeking that had occurred throughout the developed world.

1997-2007

Asylum-seekers

Unlike many other western countries, the number of those applying for asylum in Britain underwent a sharp increase in 1997 upon the return of New Labour. Their previous fall in number and subsequent rise can be seen from the following table of statistics showing annual numbers of asylum-seekers in several western democracies. Table 7.3 (p. 93) shows just how anomalous and disproportionate, relative to global figures, the increase in number has been in Britain since 1997.

The number of those gaining entry to Britain as asylum-seekers continued to increase for the first two years of the new millennium. In 2001, Britain received 71,000 new asylum applications, and, in 2002, 84,000 applications. The number of such applications has since fallen. In 2003, only 49,405 applications were received, and, in 2004, only 33,930 applications. The government claims credit for having effected this reduction through the steps it has taken to reduce the number of bogus asylum-seekers. These steps include the strengthening of border controls at points of entry in northern France, the introduction of new technologies to detect illegal entrants, and the acceleration and increase in the number of applications annually considered. In 2004, the government set itself the target of removing as many failed asylum-seekers each year as applied for asylum, a target it has met. However, the backlog of unheard applications that has accumulated since 1997 remains enormous. Moreover, even when an application is rejected, as happens in two thirds of cases, only one-fifth of failed asylum-seekers are removed from the country. As has been noted by MigrationWatch UK, an independent think-tank monitoring current migration trends to and from the UK: 'Even if the [government] target were met it would mean no inroads were being made into reducing the backlog of failed asylum seekers who number about 240,000 plus dependants.'[17]

Since 2003, there may well have been a reduction in the annual numbers of those applying for asylum in Britain, after its steep rise during the previous five years. However, since 1997, asylum-seekers have never comprised the majority of immigrants to Britain, even though, when at their height, asylum-seekers formed the single biggest group of immigrants entering Britain. There are several other immigrant groups whose numbers also have increased vastly since 1997. In aggregate, their combined number has been much greater than has been the number of asylum-seekers entering Britain in that same period. Unlike asylum-seekers, the size of each of these other groups of immigrants has increased in this period as a result of measures deliberately introduced by the government since 1997 either to encourage such an increase or at least in the knowledge it would be likely to happen as a result of such measures. Some have conjectured that the annual number of applications for asylum in Britain may well have fallen since 2003 only because it has become easier to enter the country through these other routes, and not because of any of the measures the government has introduced with the declared aim of reducing the number of asylum-seekers.

Besides those who have been able to enter or remain through applying for asylum, there are four other principal ways by which lawful entry to Britain may be gained which have all increased markedly since 1997 as a result of government policies. These are: family reunion, including marriage; full-time study; through having obtained a work permit or some other form of authorisation to work here; and, finally, EU citizenship. The increase that has come about in each of these ways will now be briefly discussed in turn, starting with family reunion and marriage.

Transcontinental arranged marriages

Shortly after assuming office in 1997, the present government honoured an electoral pledge to abolish the so-called *primary purpose rule*. This rule had previously denied entry to all non-EU citizens who had been unable to prove that their primary purpose in having married some UK resident, or for seeking to enter to do so, was not simply to gain entry and residency rights. In abolishing this rule, the government must have known it was bound to increase the number of those seeking and gaining entry having married a UK resident or in order to marry one. Abolition of the rule was one of the very few immigration-related measures the government took upon gaining office to which it had pledged itself before the 1997 election. It had possibly made this pledge to reap electoral benefit in those constituencies that contained large numbers of Pakistanis and Bengalis among whom trans-continental arranged marriage is practised on a large scale and who have been quick to take advantage of the rule's abolition.

In its five-year strategy for asylum and immigration, published in February 2005, the government undertook to end chain-migration by requiring that, in future, all settling in Britain on a family reunion basis must have to wait a further five years after so doing before being able to sponsor the settlement of any further family members.[18] For those concerned about social fragmentation consequent upon the self-segregation of minority communities in which chain-migration has been practised on a significant scale, this governmental move must be welcome. However, as has been observed by MigrationWatch UK, the government has yet to take any steps towards curb transcontinental arranged marriages which are the principal source of chain migration.

MigrationWatch UK also has noted that such marriages can be presumed to be having 'a major impact on a number of English cities'. The most notable of these are Manchester, Birmingham and Bradford. Each of them is home to a relatively large concentration of Pakistanis or Bengalis among whom this kind of marriage is especially prevalent. A report about the Bradford riots of 2001 has estimated that as many as 60 per cent of the Pakistani and Bangladeshi marriages in that town have involved a spouse who had come from Pakistan or Bangladesh.[19] As MigrationWatch UK has pointed out, the percentage of marriages of this kind among Pakistanis and Bangladeshis resident in Manchester and Birmingham is unlikely to be much different from that among each of these groups resident in Bradford. Between 1991 and 2001, the Pakistani population of Manchester grew by 48 per cent, that of Birmingham grew by 53 per cent, and that of Bradford by 46 per cent. Pakistanis now comprise four per cent, seven per cent, and ten per cent of their respective total populations. Birmingham too contains a substantial number of Bengalis whose numbers increased by 59 per cent during this period.[20] Given the much higher birth-rates of Pakistanis and Bengalis, plus their comparatively young age, should their present rate of intercontinental marriage continue, then, in a very short space of time, there is likely to occur a very large increase in the population of Britain who are either immigrants or descendants of recent immigrants. Moreover, on present showing, it is not unlikely that these new immigrants and descendants of recent immigrants will live in ever-more self-segregated and self-sufficient enclaves.

Foreign Students

As well as the number of transcontinental arranged marriages having greatly increased since the present government came into power in 1997, a substantial increase has also occurred in the number of those gaining entry to Britain from countries outside the EU as foreign students. In the six years before 1997, the numbers of those granted leave to enter Britain in such a capacity were as given in Table 7.4 (p. 84).

The number entering the country in this category has continued to rise. In 2003, the total number of foreign students stood at 319,000.[21] This increase in their number is something the government admits to favouring. Its stated grounds for so doing are that it reckons them to be 'worth some £5 billion a year to the economy... a key factor in the sustainability of many of our educational institutions, and ... [they] enable bright young people from abroad to develop lifelong ties with the UK which are of long-term benefit to the country'.[22]

Table 7.4
Annual Numbers of Foreign Students Given Leave to Enter UK
(in thousands)

1991	1992	1993	1994	1995	1996	1997	1998	1999	2000
61.1	44.8	51.9	55.0	67.2	68.2	92.8	80.7	84.9	94.6

Source: Office for National Statistics, as quoted in Browne, A., *Do We Need Mass Immigration?*, London: Civitas, 2002, p. 22.

It is open to debate whether the recent vast expansion in higher education in this country has been, on balance, a good thing for the country, rather than a monumental waste of both its human and other forms of capital. That issue is one best postponed for another occasion. However, there is some reason to doubt that those who have come in this capacity have come to study in Britain, rather than to work there.

Foreign students account for nearly half of all appli-cations for leave to enter the country with which the Managed Migration Division of the Immigration and Nationality Directorate (IND) has had to deal annually since New Labour came to power. In his account of what he has called Britain's 'Great Immigration Scandal', Steve Moxon, a former employee in that division of the IND, claims that, when vetting their applications, he found most of these applicants were not, as he had naively assumed beforehand that they would be, university students, but were 'coming here (ostensibly that is) for part-time courses, especially

English'.[23] He also claims to have discovered, when scrutinising their applications, that, in answer to the question as to how many hours of tuition per week they were coming to receive, they almost all invariably stipulated 15 hours. This is the barest minimum number of hours of study a prospective foreign student must study to qualify for full-time student status, without which they are ineligible for entry. Such facts suggest that the prime purpose of many, perhaps the majority, of such entrants has been in order to enter into paid employment here, rather than study. Moreover, spouses of foreigners granted leave to enter as foreign students also automatically become eligible to enter, and, unlike their student spouses, may lawfully work full-time. All this suggests many so-called 'full-time' foreign students, ostensibly here to learn English or something else, are in reality economic migrants. Moxon also claimed that sheer volume of work-load discouraged the IND from carrying out adequate checks on the credentials of the many language schools purporting to offer 'full-time' tuition to foreign students, as well as from verifying attendance at them of such foreign-students as purport to be receiving such tuition at them.

Labour migration

Providing inadequate scrutiny of private educational establishments purporting to cater to foreign students is, of course, something the present government would hardly admit to being official government policy. It would, however, be unable to deny it has gone out of its way deliberately to increase immigration through each of the two remaining legal channels. These are, first, the entry by non-EU citizens who have been granted a work permit or other form of authorisation so as to take up full-time employment, and, second, entry by virtue of EU citizenship.

In many ways, it has been its deliberately encouraging an increase in each of these two forms of immigration that has been the most striking and novel features of the present government's approach towards immigration. More than all the various other forms of immigration that have increased during its time in office, it has been increases from these two sources of immigration that, in recent years, have so transformed the country demographically speaking. In a jointly written article published in 2004, David Coleman, Professor of Demography at the University of Oxford, and Robert Rowthorn, Professor of Economics at the University of Cambridge, have drawn attention to what a change in official government policy has lay behind the huge increase in these two forms of immigration under the present Labour government:

> Since 1997 a new UK immigration policy has displaced previous policy aims which were focused in minimizing settlement. Large-scale immigration is now officially considered to be essential for the UK's economic well-being and beneficial for its society; measures have been introduced to increase inflows... UK immigration policy has been turned around. A restrictive policy on immigration had evolved in the late 1950s to limit the new and unexpected rise of immigration from the New Commonwealth countries ... [whose] aim has been summarised as keeping to 'an irreducible minimum the number of people coming to Britain for permanent settlement' (Home Office. Immigration and Nationality Department Annual Report 1994)... All that has changed since 1997, when the incoming Labour government began to make a decisive break with previous policies and attitudes towards immigration... The new government policy holds that regular large-scale legal immigration is essential to the continued prosperity and international competitiveness of the UK economy... In rejecting the notion that migration can or should be strictly controlled in favour of an emphasis on its benefits, a general policy of 'managed migration' thus has been adopted.[24]

The government's case for large-scale labour migration has not gone unchallenged by demographers and labour-economists such as these two authors, and by social commentators such as Anthony Browne.[25] In connection with such labour migration, it has yet to be demonstrated that it provides any but the most minimal of economic benefits for the country as a whole, as opposed to certain specific groups within it, such as employers and the well-off who find themselves provided with a source of cheap labour. The reasons claimed for need of it have turned out to be spurious. The number of unfilled vacancies in the UK has not fallen, since immigrants create their own labour demands. Economic migrants are not the solution to the problems created by Britain's ageing labour-force, since they too grow old in time. Nor can such labour immigration do much to redress the decline in Scotland's population, since practically all immigrants gravitate to the south of England. The decline in Scotland's population would be more likely to be checked, or even reversed, were net labour immigration to Britain to cease. For inward investment would then be more likely to flow to Scotland in which there is a relative surplus of labour rather than to England that would no longer serve as such a powerful magnet for internal migration from Scotland, as it has done.

Our principal concern here is only with the specific forms of immigration to Britain that have increased in consequence of the government's deliberate attempt to engineer such an increase in light of its claimed imperative economic need. It has assumed two principal forms.

First, there has been a significant increase in the amount of labour migration resulting from the government's greater willingness to issue work permits than its predecessors. In the twenty-year period between 1974 and 1994, there were only somewhere in the region of 15,000 to 30,000 such permits granted annually. Since 1997, the number issued has significantly increased. In 2003 alone, no fewer than 156,000 such permits were issued.[26]

Second, because the government believed such a form of migration to Britain would benefit the economy by meeting labour shortages, it decided to allow citizens of the eight Eastern European countries which acceded to the European Union in May 2004 to be able to work in Britain immediately from that date, rather than insisting, as have practically all the other major European Union countries, on a transitional period following accession before they could do, during which time the standard of living of their home countries could be expected to rise towards European norms, thus reducing the economic incentive for migration. The consequence of the government's decision was a huge influx into the country of workers from these new accession countries, far in excess of government forecasts.

The government originally predicted that only 15,000 Eastern Europeans from the eight New Accession countries would move to Britain each year to work there, plus whatever dependents of theirs settled as a result.[27] Based on that forecast, between May 2004 and the third quarter of 2006, the latest quarter for which there are currently any government statistics, a total of only just over 36,000 Eastern Europeans should have entered Britain to work as employees under the Worker Registration Scheme (WRS), plus their dependants. This has proved a colossal under-estimate. According to the latest Home Office statistics, over ten times that number of nationals from these countries have applied for entry: over half a million.[28] Even this head-line figure does not accurately reflect their true number and is liable to be a considerable under-estimate. This is so for two reasons. First, it does not include the number of dependants of those entering under WRS who have taken up residence in Britain since May 2004. According to Home Office statistics, the 510,000 Eastern Europeans entering under the WRS have brought with them a further 45,425 dependants.[29] This number of dependants alone is well in excess of the entire number of Eastern Europeans originally forecast to enter for purposes of work. Second, the figure of 510,000 Eastern European immigrant workers who have applied to enter Britain since May 2004 under the WRS does not include the number of Eastern Europeans coming to Britain to work in a self-employed capacity who have not been required to register before entering.

Some indication can be gained of how gross an underestimate the official head-line figure of 510,000 Eastern European immigrant workers may be from consideration of the numbers who have come from Poland. They comprise the single biggest category of Eastern Europeans from the eight new accession countries to have immigrated to Britain since May 2004. According to Home Office statistics, Poles make up 307,000 of the 510,000 Eastern European workers to have applied for entry under the WRS since May 2004, forming two-thirds of the total. When one takes account of the dependants of these Polish immigrants too, plus the unknown but sizeable number of Poles who have entered to work in a self-employed capacity, plus their dependants, then the total number of Poles to have immigrated to Britain since May 2004 is likely to exceed the total number of Eastern European workers the Home Office claims have entered under the WRS. This is certainly the view of the Polish Embassy in Britain. In February 2007, it was reported as having claimed that as many as between 500,000 and 600,000 Poles are now living in Britain.[30] This is almost double the number of Poles the Home Office reports have come under the WRS. Should Poles be representative of Eastern Europeans in general, then the consequence of the government's decision to allow nationals from the new accession countries of Eastern Europe to work in Britain immediately after May 2004 will have been to add more than a million of them to Britain's population.

The government maintains few of these labour immigrants from Eastern Europe will stay beyond a few years, but that remains to be seen. Many Huguenot refugees, who came to Britain in the seventeenth century and eventually stayed, also believed and hoped they would one day return home, as did many of the West Indians and south Asians who migrated to Britain during the 1950s. Romania and Bulgaria joined the EU at the beginning of January 2007 and the government decided not to grant their nationals the same immediate license to work here as it had done to those of the other eight Eastern European countries which preceded them into the EU. However, as many have pointed out, it remains to be seen how well it will be possible to curb their numbers. Those seeking leave to enter as self-employed will remain uncurbed. Steve Moxon claims that, in the past, the IND has demanded only the most cursory of evidence to corroborate the authenticity of the status of EU migrants who have sought entry in this way. The EU has also yet to decide whether to admit Turkey. If and when it is admitted, the same question will arise in connection with its nationals.

Illegal Immigrants

The foregoing figures concerning the recent scale of immigration to Britain do not include the very substantial numbers of illegal immigrants widely thought to be living and working in Britain, who have entered the country clandestinely or as asylum-seekers whose applications have been rejected but who have failed to leave. Since records ceased being kept in 1996 of those leaving the country, it has become notoriously difficult to form any reliable estimate as to what their number might be. Using figures from the 2001 census, an estimate of their number was produced by John Salt, director of the Migration Research Unit at University College London, upon commission from the Home Office. He estimated there were between 310,000 and 570,000 illegal immigrants in the country. This estimate, however, is widely thought to be a conservative one, since it did not include either illegal immigrants who are not in work or the dependants of the estimated illegal immigrants. Also, bearing in mind how much time has lapsed since the year on which Salt based his estimate, a more realistic estimate of their current number could be a lot higher. MigrationWatch UK has put their number somewhere between 515,000 and 870,000.[31]

Such a high estimate seems not altogether implausible in light of the following three statistical vignettes concerning illegal immigrants. First, in the course of three random days in 2001, random checks on a small percentage of vehicles entering Britain through Dover led to the discovery of nearly 300 people attempting to enter the country clandestinely.[32] Second, according to the sworn testimony of a Home Office expert in a court case in 2004, as many as between 40,000 and 50,000 Chinese were living in Manchester despite only 8,000 being recorded as doing so in the 2001 census.[33] Third, according to a recent report of the Lords and Commons Rights Committee, there are as many as 4,000 foreign women who have entered the country illegally working in brothels in Britain. They form 85 per cent of the total number of women who work in them. A decade ago, such women made up only 15 per cent of the total number of women working in British brothels.[34]

All in all, if, as was said earlier, in 1945 Britain was not yet a country of immigrants and descendants of immigrants, 60 years on, it is well on the way to becoming one.

Table 7.1
Population growth in the UK by country, 1950 and 2005 (in millions)

	1950	1960	1970	1980	1991	2001	2002	2003	2004	2005	Increase 1950-2005
Eng & Wales	44.0	45.8	48.9	49.6	50.7	52.4	52.6	52.8	53.0	53.4	9.4
Scotland	5.2	5.2	5.2	5.2	5.1	5.1	5.1	5.1	5.1	5.1	-0.1
N. Ireland	1.4	1.4	1.5	1.5	1.6	1.7	1.7	1.7	1.7	1.7	0.3
UK Total	**50.6**	**52.4**	**55.6**	**56.3**	**57.4**	**59.2**	**59.3**	**59.6**	**59.8**	**60.2**	**9.6**

Source: Statistics to 1980, Davies, N., *The Isles*, London: Papermac, 2000, p. 803; from 1991, *Population Trends*, 124, Summer 2006, Office for National Statistics.

Table 7.3
Inflows of asylum seekers into the UK and other selected western countries (in thousands)

	1991	1992	1993	1994	1995	1996	1997	1998	1999	2000
Australia	16	13	5	8	8	8	11	8	8	12
France	47	29	28	26	20	17	21	22	31	39
Germany	256	438	323	127	128	116	104	99	95	79
Italy	27	6	2	2	2	1	2	11	33	18
N'lands	22	20	35	53	29	23	34	45	43	44
UK	**73**	**32**	**28**	**42**	**55**	**37**	**42**	**58**	**91**	**98**
USA	56	104	144	147	155	128	86	55	43	52
World Total	**661**	**851**	**722**	**505**	**482**	**391**	**438**	**516**	**516**	**504**

Source: OECD 2002, *Trends in International Migration, Continuous Reporting System on Migration, 2001.* As quoted in Hughes, H., *Immigrants, Refugees and Asylum Seekers: A Global View*, St Leonards, NSW: Centre for Independent Studies, 2002, p. 39.

8

Conclusion

No one with any knowledge of the immense contribution, both economic and cultural, that immigrants and their descendants have made to Britain in the past could possibly doubt that, without it, Britain would lack much that makes it the country it is today. Indeed, much of what is thought of as quintessentially British has been contributed by them. From Punch and Judy to Madame Tussaud's, from Selfridges to Marks and Spencer, from Handel's 'Water Music' to the poetry of John Betjeman, and not least that pair of fictitious characters Ali G. and Vicky Pollard, so much of what today forms an inextricable part of the country's cultural landscape is owed to immigrants or their descendants, that it is hard to imagine how Britain might have been today were it not to have received any immigration since Norman times. Having said that, it remains the case that, until only very recently, Britain's immigrant population and hence their descendants only ever comprised a relatively small proportion of Britain's total population. It was precisely because they did that, in order to flourish in Britain, immigrants and descendants of immigrants in the past had no real alternative but to adopt its customs and manners, in their dress, language, and in innumerable other ways that did not demand they abandon anything of whatever was distinctive among the values and practices that they or their ancestors brought with them to Britain that was compatible with its culture and values.

In consequence of the mutual accommodation that in the past immigrants to Britain have been able to achieve with their host population, until only very recently, the country has enjoyed an enviable record of social harmony combined with considerable ethnic and cultural plurality. To say this is not to deny or ignore the very real tensions and conflicts that, from time to time, have soured relations between its various different ethnic groups. However, that relatively high level of social harmony the country has in the past enjoyed is now under severe threat as a result of the recent creation of varieties of cultural separation that threaten to unravel the social fabric and to disunite the country into a set of contending ethnic groups.

Those for whom this country has always been a model of tolerance and freedom cannot but have cause for deep concern about the seemingly reckless pace and scale on which immigration has recently been allowed to proceed, if not actively encouraged. As a result of it, the country may possibly have already reached a tipping point beyond which it can no longer be said to contain a single nation. Should that point have been reached, then, ironically in the course of Britain having become a nation of *immigrants*, it would have ceased to be *a nation*. Once such a point is reached, political disintegration may be predicted to be not long in following.

Some will welcome Britain's demise as a nation-state, arguing that, as a member of the European Union, its future heralds its absorption within a supra-national form of political association in which all particular national identities and allegiances of its constituent member-states become transcended and abandoned as no more than vestigial remnants of a former outmoded way of political life no longer appropriate for our age of globalisation.

Others will be of a different opinion. They will believe that, apart from within the context of nations, political cooperation and mutual civility between strangers cannot for long be maintained. Those of this latter way of thinking will be more inclined to agree with the sentiment expressed by Arthur Bryant in the epilogue of his last book:

> The legal and spiritual association of men of different creeds, callings, and classes in a nation, though often taken for granted, is a more wonderful miracle of cumulative human effort and wisdom than even the greatest achievement of science. For it enables millions who have never set eyes on one another to act together in peace and mutual trust. There can be no truer service than to preserve such a union, and prevent those millions from dissolving into antagonistic and destructive groups.[1]

In that epilogue, Bryant went on to identify, as among the most binding of this country's institutions, the British monarchy. In illustration of its binding force, this essay will conclude with a quotation that also illustrates just how well, with the appropriate will, an immigrant minority with traditions and beliefs quite different from those of the majority of Britain's population can successfully integrate and become part of the British nation without having to forfeit anything that makes it distinctive and sets it apart from others. Consider the prayer on behalf of the British royal family that Britain's Jews recite weekly in their synagogues on their Sabbath in English. Over the centuries, Jews domiciled outside their national homeland have always included such a prayer on behalf of the head of whichever state they reside in. They have done so in accordance with the divine injunction contained in a letter to their exiled community in Babylon by the prophet Jeremiah: 'Seek the welfare of the city where I have sent you into exile, and pray to the Lord on its behalf, for in its welfare you will find your welfare.'[2] In their prayer for the royal family, British Jews exhort God to bless the reigning monarch and members of the royal family, before calling upon God to 'put a spirit of wisdom and understanding into the hearts of all [the ruling sovereign's] counsellors, that they may uphold the peace of the realm, [and] advance the welfare of the nation'. The prayer ends with God being called on to 'spread the tabernacle of peace over all the dwellers on earth'.[3] In the troubled times through which the country is currently passing, I can think of no better way to end the present study than with the words of that prayer.

Save but to add one further comment. In the cause of preserving the union of which Arthur Bryant spoke, the first duty of all true patriots must be to acknowledge that, just as Britain would never have achieved all that it has done without having been a country of immigration, so too it would never have been able to achieve all this, unless its immigrants had been able to take their place within and become a part of what never has been a nation of immigrants, nor ever could become one without destroying itself in the process.

Notes

Introduction

1 Barbara Roche, Speech at IPPR Conference 'UK migration in a global economy', 11 September 2000, as reported in BBC News Online: UK Politics, *Green card 'may solve skills shortage'*, Monday, 11 September 2000.

2 *Migration: an economic and social analysis*, RDS Occasional Paper No. 6, London: Home Office, 2001, p. 7.

3 Roche, B., 'Beat the backlash', *Progress*, January /February 2004; http://www.progressives.org.uk/magazine

4 *Roots of the Future: Ethnic Diversity in the Making of Britain*, London: Commission for Racial Equality, first published 1996, revised 1997, p. 1.

5 Winder, R., *Bloody Foreigners: The Story of Immigration to Britain*, London: Little, Brown, 2004, p. x.

6 Winder, *Bloody Foreigners*, p. 2.

7 Trevelyan, G.M., *Illustrated History of England*, first published 1926, third edn London, New York and Toronto: Longman, 1956, p. xxiii.

8 Trevelyan, *Illustrated History of England*, p. 1.

3: From the Stone Age to the Roman Conquest

1 Miles, D., *The Tribes of Britain*, London: Weidenfeld and Nicolson, 2005, pp. 66-68.

2 Sykes, B., *Blood of the Isles: Exploring the Genetic Roots of Our Tribal History*, London, Toronto, Sydney, Aukland, and Johannesburg: Bantam Press, 2006, p. 10.

3 Sykes, *Blood of the Isles*, pp. 279-87, passim.

4 Oppenheimer, S., *The Origins of the British: A Genetic Detective Story* London: Constable, 2006, p. 407. The last sentence of this quotation has been moved from p. 116.

5 Miles, *The Tribes of Britain*, p. 77.

6   Pryor, F., *Britain BC: Life in Britain and Ireland Before the Romans*, first
     published 2003, London: Harper Perennial, 2004, p. 269.

7   Pryor, *Britain BC*, p. 299.

8   Pryor, *Britain BC*, p. 334.

9   James, S., *The Atlantic Celts: Ancient People or Modern Invention?*
     Madison, Wisconsin: University of Wisconsin Press, 1999,
     pp. 40-42.

10 Pryor, *Britain BC*, p. 414.

4: From the Roman Conquest to the Norman Conquest

1   Miles, D., *The Tribes of Britain*, London: Weidenfeld and Nicolson,
     2005, p. 153.

2   Miles, *The Tribes of Britain*, p. 154.

3   See Thomas, M.G., Stumpf, M.P.H. and Harke, H., 'Evidence for an
     apartheid-like social structure in early Anglo-Saxon England',
     Proceedings of the Royal Society, 2006, (doi:10.1098/rspb.206.3627).

4   Miles, *The Tribes of Britain*, pp. 176-77.

5   Sykes, B., *Blood of the Isles: Exploring the Genetic Roots of Our Tribal
     History*, London, Toronto, Sydney, Aukland, and Johannesburg:
     Bantam Press, 2006, p. 286.

5: From the Norman Conquest to the Reformation

1   Cunningham, W., *Alien Immigrants to England*, first published 1897,
     second edn, Wilson, C. (ed.), London: Frank Cass, 1969, p. 3.

2   Cunningham, *Alien Immigrants*, pp. 6-7.

3   Cunningham, *Alien Immigrants*, p. 4.

4   Cunningham, *Alien Immigrants*, p. 6.

5   Winder, R., *Bloody Foreigners: The Story of Immigration to Britain*,
     London: Little, Brown, 2004, p. 25.

6   Miles, D., *The Tribes of Britain*, London: Weidenfeld and Nicolson, 2005, p. 236.

7   Winder, *Bloody Foreigners*, p. 29.

8   Black, G., *Jewish London: An Illustrated History*, Derby: Breedon Books, 2003, p. 17.

9   See Fletcher Jones, P., *The Jews of Britain: A Thousand Years of History* Adlestrop, Gloucestershire: Windrush Press, 1990, p. 69.

10 Winder, *Bloody Foreigners*, p. 34.

11 Miles, *The Tribes of Britain*, p. 252.

12 Miles, *The Tribes of Britain*, p. 265.

13 Miles, *The Tribes of Britain*, p. 273.

14 Miles, *The Tribes of Britain*, p. 296.

15 Hinde, A., *England's Population: a History Since the Domesday Survey*, London: Hodder Arnold, 2003, p. 79.

16 Hinde, *England's Population*, p. 181.

17 Tannahill, J.A., *European Volunteer Workers in Britain*, Manchester: Manchester University Press, 1958, p. 1.

6: From the Reformation to the Second World War

1   See Winder, R., *Bloody Foreigners: The Story of Immigration to Britain*, London: Little, Brown, 2004, p. 229.

2   Miles, D., *The Tribes of Britain*, London: Weidenfeld and Nicolson, 2005, p. 311.

3   Winder, *Bloody Foreigners*, p. 100.

4   King, T.E., Parkin, E.J., Swinfield, G., Cruciani, F., Scozzari, R., Rosa, A., Lim, S.K., Xue, Y., Tyler-Smith, C. and Jobling, M.A., 'Africans in Yorkshire? The deepest-rooting clade of the Y phylogeny within an English genealogy', *European Journal of Human Genetics*, 2007, 15, 288-293; published online 24 January 2007.

5   Ballard, R., 'The South Asian Presence in Britain and its Transnational Connections' in Parekh, B., Singh, G. and Vertovec,

S., *Culture and Economy in the Indian Diaspora,* London: Routledge, 2003.

6   Gwynn, R., *Huguenot Heritage: The History and Contribution of the Huguenots in Britain,* second revised edn, Brighton and Portland, Oregon: Sussex Academic Press, 2001, p. 2, footnote 2.

7   Gwynn, *Huguenot Heritage,* pp. 190-91.

8   Walvin, J., *Passage to Britain: Immigration in British History and Politics,* Harmondsworth: Penguin Books, 1984, p. 27.

9   Fletcher Jones, P., *The Jews of Britain: A Thousand Years of History* Adlestrop, Gloucestershire: Windrush Press, 1990, p. 148.

10 Cunningham, W., *Alien Immigrants to England,* first published 1897, second edn, Wilson, C. (ed.), London: Frank Cass, 1969, p. 255.

11 Black, G., *Jewish London: An Illustrated History,* Derby: Breedon Books, 2003, p. 78.

12 Cesarani, D., 'The Changing Character of Citizenship and Nationality', in Cesarani, D. and Fulbrook, M., *Citizenship, Nationality and Migration in Europe,* London and New York: Routledge, 1996, pp. 57-73, p. 62.

13 Coleman, D., 'U.K. Statistics on Immigration: Development and Limitations' *International Migration Review,* 21, 1987, pp. 1138-1169, p. 1145.

14 Quoted in White, J., *Rothschild Building: Life in an East End Tenement Block 1887-1920,* first published 1980, Pimlico edn, London: Pimlico, 2003, p. 17.

15 Black, *Jewish London,* p. 88.

16 Walvin, *Passage to Britain,* p. 65.

17 Tannahill, J.A., *European Volunteer Workers in Britain,* Manchester: Manchester University Press, 1958, p. 1.

18 Winder, *Bloody Foreigners,* p. 215.

19 Winder, *Bloody Foreigners,* p. 215.

20 Winder, *Bloody Foreigners,* p. 216.

21 Winder, *Bloody Foreigners,* p. 226.

22 Winder, *Bloody Foreigners*, p. 246.

23 Ballard, 'The South Asian Presence in Britain and its Transnational Connections'.

24 Walvin, *Passage to Britain*, pp. 90-101 *passim*.

7: From the Second World War to the Present

1 Source: 'Foreign-born', Office for National Statistics, 15 December 2005.

2 Source: 'International Migration', Office for National Statistics, 24 June 2004.

3 Source: 'International Migration', Office for National Statistics, 15 December 2005.

4 Source: 'Population Change', Office for National Statistics, 24 August 2006.

5 Paxman, J., *The English: A Portrait of a People,* London: Michael Joseph, 1998, pp. 72-73.

6 Norfolk, A., 'How bombers' town is turning into an enclave of isolationists', *The Times,* 21 October 2006.

7 Browne, A., 'UK whites will be minority by 2100', *Observer,* 3 September 2000.

8 Figures from Linsell, T., *An English Nationalism,* Norfolk: Athelney, 2001, pp. 414-15.

9 Tannahill, J.A., *European Volunteer Workers in Britain*, Manchester: Manchester University Press, 1958, p.1.

10 Tannahill, *European Volunteer Workers in Britain*, p., 5.

11 Tannahill, *European Volunteer Workers in Britain*, p. 4.

12 Tannahill, *European Volunteer Workers in Britain*, pp. 5-6.

13 Tannahill, *European Volunteer Workers in Britain*, p. 6.

14 Figures derived from Peach, C., Introduction to C. Peach, C. (ed.), *Ethnicity in the 1991 Census. Vol. 2: The Ethnic Minority Populations of Great Britain,* London: HMSO, 1991, p. 8.

15 Ballard, R., 'The South Asian Presence in Britain and its Transnational Connections' in Parekh, B., Singh, G. and Vertovec, S., *Culture and Economy in the Indian Diaspora*, London: Routledge, 2003, sec. 2.2.

16 Winder, R., *Bloody Foreigners: The Story of Immigration to Britain*, London: Little, Brown, 2004, p. 321, footnote.

17 'An overview of UK migration', MigrationWatch UK Briefing Paper, revised 3 January 2006.

18 See *Controlling our borders: Making migration work for Britain - Five year strategy for asylum and immigration*, Norwich: The Stationery Office, 2005, p. 22, para. 39.

19 Appendix 7 of Lord Ousley's report into disturbances in Bradford, 'Race Relations in Bradford' by Mahony, G.V., cited in 'The impact of chain migration', MigrationWatch UK, 5 April 2005.

20 'The impact of chain migration', MigrationWatch UK, 5 April 2005.

21 *Controlling our borders*, p. 15, para. 16.

22 *Controlling our borders*, p. 15, para. 16.

23 Moxon, S., *The Great Immigration Scandal*, First published 2004, Second edn, Exeter: Imprint Academic, 2006, p. 140.

24 Coleman, D. and Rowthorn, R., 'The Economic Effects of Immigration into the United Kingdom', *Population and Development Review*, 30, 4 (2004), pp. 579-624., pp. 579-81. I have transposed the final sentence from p. 580.

25 Browne, A., *Do We Need Mass Immigration?*, London: Civitas, 2002.

26 'An overview of UK migration', MigrationWatch UK, p. 3.

27 '"Nearly 600,000" new EU migrants', BBC News Website, 28 August 2006; http://news.bbc.co.uk/go/pr/fr/-/1/hi/uk_politics/5273356.stm

28 'Accession Monitoring Report: May 2004-September 2006'; Home Office online report published 21 November 2006. Table 1, p. 5.

29 'Accession Monitoring Report: May 2004-September 2006'; Home Office online report published 21 November 2006. Table 1, p. 5 and Table 4, p. 12.

30 'Twice as many Poles living in Britain than officials think', *The Times*, 10 February 2007.
http://www.timesonline.co.uk/tol/news/uk/article1361951.ece

31 'An overview of UK migration' MigrationWatch UK, p. 2.

32 See Moxton, *The Great Immigration Scandal*, p. 9.

33 See Moxton, *The Great Immigration Scandal*, p. 148.

34 Source of information: 'Sex trafficking up', *The Times*, 13 October 2006.

8: Conclusion

1 Bryant, Sir Arthur, *Spirit of England*, first published 1982, London: House of Stratus, 2001, p. 198.

2 Jeremiah 29.7, RSV.

3 *The Authorised Daily Prayer Book of the United Hebrew Congregation of the British Empire*, trans. Singer, S., 24th edn, London: Eyre and Spottiswood, 1956, p. 156.